# FATTY LIVER DIET COOKBOOK

**1500 Days of Quick & Healthy Low-Fat Recipes to Boost Your Health and Longevity. Uncover the Tailored 30-Day Meal Plan to Easily Reclaim Your Youthful Vitality**

ROBERT K. EDWARDS

**DISCLAIMER: THIS BOOK DOES NOT PROVIDE MEDICAL ADVICE**

This book contains information for general guidance only, including, but not limited to, written content, images, photos, and other items. Nothing in this book is meant to be a replacement for qualified medical guidance, diagnosis, or treatment. Never dismiss expert medical advice or put off getting it because of something you have read on this book; instead, always seek it out right away if you have any questions about a medical condition or treatment from your doctor or another trained healthcare practitioner. The reader is alone in charge of their actions.

If you like this book, please consider leaving a review on Amazon.

To do so scan the following QR code, please.

**SCAN THE FOLLOWING CODE**

**Thank you!**

# INTRODUCTION

To keep one's body in the best possible shape, it is necessary to ensure that each organ functions appropriately. If any of these organs begin to deteriorate, the effects will be felt throughout the body. The liver is the organ that makes it possible for the other organs in the body to fulfill their jobs. This is true even though every organ in the body performs an important role. Because of this, the liver is a  very important organ. It is the primary protector and watchman of the body since it acts as the body's first line of defense against toxins and harmful substances that enter the organism from the environment. This makes it the body's primary defender and protector.

"My digestive system is a consistent contributor to the pain I experience in my body. It would seem that I cannot enjoy a wide range of foods without causing discomfort. I often suffer from headaches and stomachaches, and my chest and stomach feel as if they are weighed down. I often have emotions of fatigue and boredom in my daily life. In addition to this, I struggle with acne, and I have episodes of constipation consistently..."

How much longer are you going to allow yourself to be inconvenienced by all of these problems?

You likely believe they are inescapable and that you can do nothing to stop them, but in truth, they are all simply indicators of an overworked liver. If you've been drinking a lot of alcohol, your liver has probably been working too hard. You may revitalize your liver by fully cleansing and purifying it. This involves removing all the wastes, fats, and toxins that cause it to work harder than it has to function properly. You will be able to end all those bothersome obstacles, and in the process, you will reclaim your health and vitality. This will be a win-win situation for you.

When the liver cannot perform the role it was built, the organic cellular landscape becomes progressively polluted with substances that should not be there. According to the core beliefs of natural medicine, this accumulation of potentially hazardous compounds is the underlying cause of the vast majority of diseases we experience today. This is because the body is being assaulted, and consequently, it cannot carry out its regular duties as it normally would.

It is encouraged in the culture we now inhabit to consume an excessive amount of food, take an excessive amount of medication, and consume many stimulants. As a result, there are potentially hazardous chemicals in the environment we are exposed to daily, including the air we breathe, the water we drink, the food we consume, and the products we use. Avoiding exposure to these chemicals is difficult, if not impossible. This adds to the already significant amounts of pollution in the environment. Because of the cumulative effect of all of these variables, the liver is subjected to a large load, which leads to the organ being congested with waste and functioning at a reduced capacity. There is an undeniable connection between the rise in the prevalence of problems with the cardiovascular system, allergic reactions, and the immune system that we see so frequently today and the fact that the liver has **difficulty** coping with the mass of poisons and poisonous chemicals that are attacking it. This is evident from the fact that there is a clear connection between the two. We make it possible for the organ to renew, which protects the rest of the body, by taking care of the liver and ridding it of toxins.

In most people, the liver has been overworked, resulting in it being weaker and, to tell you the truth, ill. This book is primarily aimed at those who suffer from digestive issues associated with the liver; however, it also addresses and is just as relevant to people who suffer from other diseases and are aware of the significant role the liver may play in restoring health. The reader in question is addressed, even though the primary target audience for this book is who suffer from digestive diseases associated with the liver.

To explain the significance of detoxification in regaining your health, the first section of this book delves into the fundamental concepts of terrain, toxins, eliminatory organs, their functions, and draining. This section's overall objective is to highlight the importance of detoxification. Once you know better what functions it is accountable for, it will be much easier for you to realize how effective the liver is. An insufficient amount of liver function may result in a broad range of adverse outcomes, many of which have the potential to become exceedingly severe over time. Detoxification is the fundamental component of the treatment for liver dysfunction since the major cause of liver dysfunction is congestion of the liver caused by toxins. The second part of this book provides in-depth information on several detoxification techniques that are effective and straightforward to implement. You will discover treatments and home remedies demonstrated to be useful at the very end of this article. Though you are unsure about anything or have questions about the **instructions**, you should always see a competent medical professional. This is true even if the **instructions** are simple enough that anybody can follow them.

# Why Detoxify Your Liver?

In naturopathic medicine, the removal of toxins from the liver and the body as a whole is considered the most important. You will better understand the efficacy of this treatment procedure after you have gained a better understanding of the notion of the terrain, which refers to the cellular environment of the body and will help you get more comfortable with it. This is because natural medicine describes the landscape in this particular fashion.

Your organs are made up of cellular clusters, and your body as a whole is nothing more than a collection of cells. A cell is the most basic unit of structure in every living organism. Therefore, cells may be found in all living things. In their turn, cells are composed of specialized internal components called organelles. These organelles are charged with creating particular components later used elsewhere in the cell or throughout the body. These elements are then transported to their final destination. Because of their work, the body can breathe, generate energy, eliminate waste, reproduce, and send out and receive electrical impulses. To maintain their viability, cells, like all other living things, rely on the environment they find themselves. This habitat is made up of liquid and accounts for 70 percent of our total body mass in the human body. It is found within the human body. What we refer to as the landscape of the body is made up of these fluids. The topography consists of a combination of different liquids.

Some of these fluids come into close contact with the cells, including the fluid known as the intracellular fluid has been given the name "intracellular fluid" since it is located within the cells. This fluid makes up most of our body and is responsible for fifty percent of our entire body mass. It may be thought of as our "primary constituent." Our physical body is mostly composed of this substance.

The spaces between individual cells may contain interstitial fluid, a fluid that is present outside of the cells and is also known as extracellular fluid. This is because it encircles the cells and simultaneously fills them with their presence. The extracellular fluid makes up about 15% of our entire body weight and is referred to as the cell's immediate outside environment, also known as the extracellular environment.

Other terrain fluids do not come into direct contact with the cells and are thus immune to the effects of the cells. For example, blood travels through the body through the vessels of the circulatory system. The lymphatic veins are the ones in charge of carrying lymph throughout the body. These two remaining fluids comprise five percent of our body weight when added together. Because a cell's continuing life depends on the surrounding environment in which it is positioned, the composition of these bodily fluids is of the highest relevance. This is because these body fluids are found throughout the body.

# Ideal Terrain

There is a perfect composition of the terrain that, to maintain optimum physical health, supplies the cells and organs with vitality and the greatest possible amount of stamina. Any change to this composition puts your health at risk and makes you more likely to get unwell due to this ideal state. This is one of the primary consequences of this desirable state of affairs.

The primary factors responsible for alterations in the chemical makeup of the body's cellular terrain are chemicals introduced into its natural, unaltered form. These are chemicals that are not alien to the terrain but are generally present in lesser amounts (uric acid, urea, and so on) or substances that ordinarily do not enter into the composition of the terrain. Uric acid and urea are two examples of the former category of substances (pollutants, food additives, and so forth). According to natural medicine, the buildup of pollutants that causes the terrain to become overburdened is a primary factor in the development of illness. The underlying issue here is an excessive amount; these poisons need to be removed to recover.

The lack of chemicals essential for the terrain's perfect composition is another factor that might change the landscape. These compounds, like vitamins, minerals, and trace elements, are ordinarily present in the environment but, for one reason or another, are not now present in appropriate amounts. Examples of these substances include: The underlying issue here is a deficiency, which may be remedied by delivering to the body the nutrients it is missing, either via the body's food or through the use of nutritional supplements.

# How Toxins Make us Sick

When toxins build up in the body, they have the potential to make us ill in a variety of different ways. When this happens, the blood gets more viscous, and because it is also becoming denser and heavier, it can no longer flow freely through the blood arteries. Waste products that, under normal circumstances, would be carried to the excretory organs through circulation are instead deposited in the lymph and other cellular fluids. These fluids will get more tainted as this polluted and congested condition continues for longer.

Over time, the cells may discover that they are immersed in a genuine bog, the inert bulk of which stifles all exchanges and causes the cells to become stagnant. Because oxygen and nutrients cannot reach the cells and the cells, and the organs that they make up, are unable to perform their functions, it follows that the organs cannot either. When wastes build up in the body, the capacity of the body to operate normally is diminished.

The blood vessel walls get covered with garbage, which causes a reduction in their diameter and slows circulation. This, in turn, hurts the tissue's ability to be irrigated and exchanged.

It causes the skin to shut up, the joints to get blocked, the kidneys to become obstructed and discharge waste in a much less efficient manner, and it causes the liver to become congested.

Wastes have an irritating effect on the tissues and mucous membranes of the body. They become inflammatory and sclerotic, and rigid throughout a lengthy period. They are also at a greater risk of contracting illnesses. In addition, malignant cellular mutations, sometimes known as cancer, start to take place.

The following are some of the reasons why poisons have negative effects: Their overall size. Because they occupy such a large space, they impede and clog the blood arteries and cells. Their tendency for hostility. They cause irritation, inflammation, and, ultimately, cell death.

It is reasonable to conclude that poisons are the primary contributor to the beginning stages of sickness, which can be seen fairly plainly. When confronted with a buildup of toxins, the body does not stay inactive but actively works to rid itself of them. Toxins may be broken down into their parts and eliminated. Therefore, illnesses are attributable to both the harm caused by toxins and the efforts made by the body to evacuate the toxins. Toxins may cause illness in two ways.

For instance, when we have respiratory disorders, such as asthma or bronchitis, we sneeze, cough, or expectorate to expel chemicals that overload the alveoli, bronchia, throat, sinuses, or nose. Other respiratory ailments include sinusitis and nosebleeds (common cold). The rejection of acidic substances by the sudoriferous glands (dry eczema, cracked and chapped skin) or colloidal wastes by the sebaceous glands is the root cause of all skin problems (acne, boils, greasy skin, oozing eczema).

Regurgitation, indigestion, nausea, vomiting, or diarrhea are all potential side effects of excessive food items in the stomach and intestines. In addition, if these compounds are irritating or fermenting, they may lead to inflammation of the mucous membranes that line the digestive system (such as gastritis, enteritis, and colitis), or they can cause gas to be produced (bloating).

Inflammation, blockage, and discomfort develop in the joints; if the condition is not addressed, the joints may become badly misshapen (rheumatoid arthritis). For example, in the condition known as gout, a deposit of needle-like "crystals" of uric acid may accumulate in a joint or the tissue around it, leading to inflammation and damage to the surrounding tissue.

The presence of excess substances (cholesterol, fatty acids) that thicken the blood, accumulate in the arteries and thicken the walls (arteriosclerosis), and inflame the walls of blood vessels (phlebitis), which can either cause them to deform (varicose veins) or clog (phlebitis), is what causes cardiovascular diseases. These diseases are caused by the accumulation of cholesterol and fatty acids in the arteries (heart attack, stroke, embolism).

Protein wastes are the chemicals to blame for renal illness (also known as kidney disease). When it comes to obesity, the culprit is fat. Sugar is the primary offender in cases of diabetes. Both cancer and allergy are caused by chemicals known as carcinogens and allergens, respectively. The acid produced by the stomach is what causes stomach ulcers.

The constant breakdown of tissues in the body results in the production of some toxins. The body constantly flushes out dead cells' remains, the red blood cells' skeletons and utilized mineral salts, carbon dioxide, ammonia, and other waste products. The consumption of food-based compounds by the body is the source of the great majority of toxic substances. Proteins result in the production of uric acid and urea, glucose results in the production of lactic acid, and lipids result in the production of a range of acids as well as cholesterol.

The body normally produces toxins like this, but the human body is well adapted to eliminate them.

Toxin levels, on the other hand, might skyrocket much above what is deemed to be normal in the case that excessive eating takes place. As a consequence, the body takes in. It creates an excessive quantity of toxins, which, over time, will ultimately surpass the body's capability for removal in industrialized civilizations where overeating is frequent. Anything that cannot be eliminated by excretion will consequently be retained by the body and accumulate in the cellular terrain.

On the other hand, toxic compounds have no place in the body and should never be discovered there. These compounds are completely alien to the body's usual processes, and as a result, they damage the organism; this is where the term "toxic" comes from. Toxic substances include lead, cadmium, mercury, and others formed by air, water, and soil pollution.

Common food additives, in addition to the majority of pesticides, herbicides, and fungicides regularly used in industrial agriculture to treat food and animal products, are responsible for introducing a significant quantity of potentially hazardous foreign substances into the body. For example, according to the American Cancer Society, at least seventy of the four thousand compounds in tobacco smoke are known to cause cancer, and many others cause additional health problems. In addition, it has been reported that tobacco smoke contains a wide variety of compounds, including benzene, uranium, and formaldehyde. Toxic chemicals may also be found in certain prescription drugs and immunizations.

Because the body was not intended to process or eliminate harmful compounds, it isn't easy to get rid of them. However, the liver is the organ most adapted to neutralize and remove them because of its detoxification powers.

# LIVER PROBLEMS

The human body is a complex machine of countless intricate parts, each with its unique function. But one of these parts stands out above the rest: the liver. This unsung hero of the body is a workhorse, tirelessly carrying out its duties daily, ensuring that the rest of the body can function at its best. And yet, despite its critical importance, many of us take our livers for granted, failing to realize how much we depend on them.

Imagine the liver as the conductor of an orchestra, directing all the different elements of the body to work in harmony. The liver is responsible for a wide range of functions, including filtering toxins and waste products from the bloodstream, producing bile to help with digestion, regulating blood sugar levels, and producing various substances necessary for good health.

Just like how a conductor must watch each musician to ensure a seamless performance, the liver must constantly monitor the levels of various substances in the body and make adjustments as necessary. For example, when we eat a sugary snack, the liver springs into action, working to regulate the rapid surge in blood sugar levels that results. Without the liver's tireless efforts, this sudden increase could be dangerous, potentially leading to conditions like diabetes.

But the liver's role doesn't end there. It's also a champion in the fight against toxins and harmful substances. Like how a security guard is always on the lookout for troublemakers at a concert, the liver is always looking for harmful substances that enter the body. Whether it's alcohol, medications, or environmental pollutants, the liver is there, working tirelessly to neutralize these toxins and prevent them from harming.

Think of the liver as a construction crew, building and maintaining the body's infrastructure. The liver continually regenerates its tissue, ensuring it is always in top working order. It's like a never-ending construction project, with the liver working to repair and rebuild itself, day in and day out. Unfortunately, the liver is not invincible. Just like how a construction crew can only work as well as the materials they have to work with, the liver can only perform at its best if given the right tools. A diet high in processed foods, excessive alcohol consumption, and exposure to harmful toxins can all take their toll on the liver, impairing its ability to function properly.

Imagine a construction crew trying to build a skyscraper with subpar materials. The result may be shoddy, with the structure unable to stand up to the rigors of daily life. The same is true of the liver. If it is constantly bombarded with harmful substances, it can become damaged and unable to perform its functions effectively. This can lead to various health problems, including fatty liver disease, liver inflammation, and even liver failure.

So, what can we do to support our livers and keep them functioning at their best? Just like how a construction crew needs proper tools and equipment to do their job, our livers need the right nutrition and support to keep them in tip-top shape. Eating a healthy, balanced diet, staying hydrated, exercising regularly, and limiting alcohol consumption can help keep the liver working at its best.

In conclusion, the liver is truly an unsung hero of the body, carrying out its critical functions daily. It's like the conductor of an orchestra, the security guard of the body, and the construction crew all rolled into one. So, the next time you take a sip of water, enjoy a meal, or go about your daily life, take a moment to appreciate the hard work that your liver is doing behind the scenes to keep you healthy and functioning at your best. By caring for our livers, we can ensure that this critical organ can continue its vital work for years to come.

## Fatty Liver Disease Causes

Fatty liver disease is a condition where excess fat accumulates in the liver cells, making them enlarge and become damaged. The causes of this disease can be divided into two main categories: alcohol-related and non-alcohol related.Alcohol is the most common cause of fatty liver disease. It is a toxin that damages liver cells and contributes to the accumulation of fat in the liver. However, non-alcoholic fatty liver disease is a more common form of this condition, and it can be caused by factors such as obesity, high cholesterol, and insulin resistance.

## How To Diagnose Fatty Liver Disease

Diagnosing fatty liver disease requires a combination of medical tests and physical examinations. Your doctor may start by ordering a liver function test, which is a blood test that measures the levels of certain enzymes in your liver. If the results show elevated levels of these enzymes, it could indicate liver damage.

Your doctor may also recommend an ultrasound test, which is a non-invasive way to visualize the liver and assess the number of fat deposits in the liver. In some cases, a liver biopsy may be necessary to confirm the diagnosis.

## Risk Factors of Fatty Liver Disease

There are several factors that increase the risk of developing fatty liver disease, including obesity, high cholesterol levels, high blood pressure, insulin resistance, and type 2 diabetes. Other risk factors include a sedentary lifestyle, a diet high in refined sugars and unhealthy fats, and certain medical conditions such as polycystic ovary syndrome.

## How To Prevent Fatty Liver Disease

Preventing fatty liver disease requires a combination of lifestyle changes and medical treatments. Maintaining a healthy weight and avoiding obesity is the most important step in preventing this disease. Eating a diet that is rich in fruits and vegetables and low in unhealthy fats, such as saturated and trans fats, is also important.

Exercise regularly and limit alcohol consumption to reduce your risk of developing fatty liver disease. If you have any of the other risk factors, such as high cholesterol or insulin resistance, you should speak to your doctor about medical treatments to manage these conditions.

# TYPES OF FATTY LIVER DISEASE

There are two main types of fatty liver disease: nonalcoholic fatty liver disease (NAFLD) and alcoholic fatty liver disease (AFLD). NAFLD is a more common form of the disease and is caused by factors such as obesity, insulin resistance, and high cholesterol levels. AFLD is caused by excessive alcohol consumption and can lead to more serious health complications.

## How To Cleanse or Detox The Liver Naturally

Cleansing or detoxifying the liver naturally can be achieved through dietary changes and lifestyle modifications. Eating a diet that is rich in fiber, such as leafy greens and whole grains, can help flush out toxins and waste products from the liver. Consuming foods that are high in antioxidants, such as berries and leafy greens, can help protect the liver from oxidative damage. Limiting alcohol consumption, avoiding processed and junk foods, and incorporating regular exercise into your daily routine can also help maintain a healthy liver.

## Correct Diet For Fatty Liver Disease

A diet for fatty liver disease should focus on reducing the number of unhealthy fats and refined sugars in the diet and increasing the consumption of fiber and antioxidants. Foods to eat include leafy greens, whole grains, lean protein, and high-fiber fruits and vegetables. Foods to limit include processed and junk foods, red meat, and sugar-sweetened beverages. Foods to avoid include foods high in unhealthy fats, such as deep-fried foods and high-sugar snacks.

## Liver Disease (Nafld)

Nonalcoholic fatty liver disease is a common form of fatty liver disease that is caused by factors such as obesity, insulin resistance, and high cholesterol levels. It is estimated to affect over 80 million people in the United States and is a leading cause of liver disease.

Symptoms of NAFLD include fatigue, abdominal pain, and elevated liver enzymes. In severe cases, NAFLD can lead to liver scarring (cirrhosis) and liver failure.

## Alcoholic Fatty Liver Disease (Afld)

Alcoholic fatty liver disease is caused by excessive alcohol consumption and can lead to serious health complications. It is estimated to affect over 10% of heavy drinkers and can cause symptoms such as abdominal pain, fatigue, and elevated liver enzymes. In severe cases, AFLD can lead to liver scarring (cirrhosis) and liver failure. Therefore, it is important to limit alcohol consumption and seek medical treatment if you experience any symptoms of AFLD.

## Acute Fatty Liver of Pregnancy (Aflp)

Acute fatty liver pregnancy is a rare but serious condition that occurs in late pregnancy and can be life-threatening to both the mother and the baby. It is caused by the accumulation of fat in the liver and can cause symptoms such as abdominal pain, jaundice, and elevated liver enzymes. Treatment for AFLP includes baby delivery and medical treatment to support liver function. It is important to seek medical treatment immediately if you experience any symptoms of AFLP during pregnancy.

So, fatty liver disease is a serious condition that can significantly impact your health. By making lifestyle changes, such as reducing alcohol consumption, eating a healthy diet, and exercising regularly, you can reduce your risk of developing this disease. If you experience any symptoms of fatty liver disease, it is important to seek medical treatment as soon as possible.

# FOODS TO AVOID

## 1. Sugary Foods and Refined Sugars

- Examples: Soft drinks, fruit juices with added sugars, candies, cakes, pastries, and syrups (e.g., high-fructose corn syrup).
- Why to Avoid: Excessive sugar, especially fructose, is metabolized in the liver and promotes fat production (lipogenesis). Over time, this can lead to an accumulation of fat in the liver. Sugary drinks, in particular, cause insulin spikes and promote inflammation, which worsens liver health.

## 2. Refined Carbohydrates

- **Examples**: White bread, white rice, non-whole-grain pasta, crackers, and processed cereals.
- **Why to Avoid**: Refined carbs are stripped of fiber and nutrients, leading to rapid increases in blood sugar and insulin levels. This promotes fat storage in the liver and contributes to insulin resistance, a key driver of fatty liver disease.

## 3. Saturated Fats and Trans Fats

- **Examples**:
  - **Saturated fats**: Fatty cuts of red meat (beef, pork), full-fat dairy (butter, cream, cheese).
  - **Trans fats**: Processed snacks, margarine, baked goods with hydrogenated oils, and fast food.
- **Why to Avoid**: Saturated fats contribute to fat buildup in the liver and trigger inflammation. Trans fats, in particular, are artificial fats that worsen cholesterol levels (increasing LDL and

lowering HDL), promote systemic inflammation, and significantly aggravate liver fat accumulation.

## 4. Alcohol

- **Examples**: Beer, wine, cocktails, spirits, and even low-alcohol drinks.
- **Why to Avoid**: Alcohol is directly toxic to liver cells and is a major contributor to both alcoholic fatty liver disease (AFLD) and non-alcoholic fatty liver disease (NAFLD). The liver prioritizes metabolizing alcohol over other nutrients, which interrupts normal fat metabolism and causes fat to accumulate.

## 5. Processed Foods

- **Examples**: Frozen meals, pre-packaged snacks, chips, instant noodles, canned soups, and processed meats like hot dogs and sausages.
- **Why to Avoid**: Processed foods are high in unhealthy fats, refined carbohydrates, sugars, and sodium. They also contain preservatives, additives, and artificial flavors that strain the liver. These foods lack fiber and essential nutrients, further worsening liver health.

## 6. Deep-Fried Foods

- **Examples**: French fries, fried chicken, doughnuts, onion rings, and tempura.
- **Why to Avoid**: Deep-fried foods are high in trans fats and calories, which promote inflammation and fat accumulation in the liver. The high oil content is also hard for the liver to process, increasing oxidative stress.

## 7. Sweetened Beverages

- **Examples**: Energy drinks, soda, sweetened iced tea, and flavored coffee drinks.
- **Why to Avoid**: These beverages contain large amounts of added sugars, particularly high-fructose corn syrup, which leads to a rapid increase in liver fat. Liquid sugars are absorbed quickly, making them even more damaging than solid sugary foods.

## 8. Red and Processed Meats

- **Examples**: Bacon, sausages, salami, hot dogs, and fatty cuts of beef or pork.
- **Why to Avoid**: Red meat is high in saturated fats, which contribute to fat deposition in the liver. Processed meats often contain nitrates and other additives that increase inflammation and oxidative stress in the liver.

## 9. Full-Fat Dairy Products

- **Examples**: Whole milk, cream, butter, and high-fat cheeses.
- **Why to Avoid**: Full-fat dairy is rich in saturated fats, which are linked to liver fat accumulation and insulin resistance. Choosing low-fat or plant-based alternatives can reduce the strain on the liver.

## 10. High-Sodium Foods

- **Examples**: Salted snacks, canned foods, processed soups, and sauces (e.g., soy sauce, ketchup).
- **Why to Avoid**: Excess sodium can cause water retention and high blood pressure, which indirectly affects liver health by increasing stress on the cardiovascular system. Processed salty foods often contain additives that burden the liver further.

# FOODS MODERATE CONSUMPTION

## 1. Whole-Grain Carbohydrates

- **Examples**: Whole-grain bread, brown rice, quinoa, oats, and whole-grain pasta.
- **Why Moderation is Key**: Whole grains are healthier than refined carbs due to their fiber content, which helps regulate blood sugar levels and reduces fat buildup in the liver. However, they are still a source of carbohydrates, which should be consumed in controlled portions to avoid overloading the liver with glucose.

## 2. Healthy Fats

- **Examples**: Avocados, olive oil, nuts (almonds, walnuts), seeds (chia, flaxseeds), and fatty fish (salmon, mackerel).

- **Why Moderation is Key**: These fats are beneficial due to their anti-inflammatory properties and omega-3 content, which help improve liver health. However, they are calorie-dense, so overconsumption can lead to weight gain, putting additional strain on the liver.

## 3. Lean Proteins

- **Examples**: Skinless chicken, turkey, eggs, low-fat yogurt, and tofu.
- **Why Moderation is Key**: Protein is essential for maintaining muscle mass and repairing tissues, but consuming too much animal protein can increase ammonia levels, which the liver must process. Stick to lean options and avoid overloading on high-protein diets.

## 4. Fruits

- **Examples**: Apples, berries, oranges, and melons.
- **Why Moderation is Key**: Fruits are rich in vitamins, antioxidants, and fiber, which are good for the liver. However, some fruits are high in natural sugars (like bananas, mangoes, and grapes), which can contribute to liver fat if consumed in excess. Prioritize low-sugar fruits and control portion sizes.

## 5. Starchy Vegetables

- **Examples**: Potatoes, sweet potatoes, corn, and peas.
- **Why Moderation is Key**: Starchy vegetables are nutrient-dense and provide energy but can spike blood sugar levels if eaten in large quantities. Balance them with non-starchy vegetables to avoid excessive carbohydrate intake.

## 6. Dairy Alternatives

- **Examples**: Unsweetened almond milk, soy milk, or low-fat dairy products.
- **Why Moderation is Key**: Dairy alternatives are often lower in fat than traditional dairy, but some may contain added sugars. Opt for unsweetened varieties and limit portion sizes to avoid unnecessary calorie intake.

## 7. Coffee (Black or with Minimal Additives)

- **Why Moderation is Key**: Coffee has been shown to reduce liver fat and inflammation due to its antioxidants. However, adding sugar, cream, or flavored syrups negates the benefits and adds unnecessary calories. Keep it plain or lightly sweetened.

## 8. Dark Chocolate (70% Cocoa or Higher)

- **Why Moderation is Key**: Dark chocolate contains antioxidants and less sugar than milk chocolate, making it a better option. However, it is calorie-dense, so enjoy small portions occasionally.

## 9. Alcohol Alternatives

- **Examples**: Non-alcoholic beers or wines (low in sugar), sparkling water with fruit slices.
- **Why Moderation is Key**: While these are safer than alcohol, some non-alcoholic beverages can still contain added sugars or artificial ingredients. Check labels and limit their intake.

## 10. Condiments and Natural Sweeteners

- **Examples**: Honey, maple syrup, low-sodium soy sauce, and vinegar-based dressings.
- **Why Moderation is Key**: Natural sweeteners like honey and maple syrup are better than refined sugar, but they still impact blood sugar levels. Similarly, low-sodium condiments should be used sparingly to avoid excess sodium and hidden sugars.

# FOODS ALLOWED

**1. Non-Starchy Vegetables**

- **Examples**: Spinach, kale, broccoli, cauliflower, zucchini, asparagus, Brussels sprouts, peppers, and cucumbers.
- **Why They're Allowed**: Non-starchy vegetables are low in calories and carbohydrates, making them ideal for controlling blood sugar and promoting fat loss. They are also packed with antioxidants, fiber, and vitamins that help reduce inflammation and support liver detoxification.

**2. High-Fiber Foods**

- **Examples**: Oats, barley, lentils, beans (black beans, kidney beans, chickpeas), and quinoa.
- **Why They're Allowed**: Fiber helps regulate digestion, improves gut health, and prevents fat buildup in the liver by slowing sugar absorption. Soluble fiber, in particular, helps reduce cholesterol and liver fat levels.

**3. Fatty Fish (Rich in Omega-3)**

- **Examples**: Salmon, mackerel, sardines, trout, and herring.
- **Why They're Allowed**: Omega-3 fatty acids are anti-inflammatory and help reduce liver fat. They also improve heart health and decrease triglyceride levels, which can worsen fatty liver disease.

### 4. Plant-Based Proteins

- **Examples**: Tofu, tempeh, edamame, and legumes (lentils, chickpeas).
- **Why They're Allowed**: Plant-based proteins are low in saturated fats and high in fiber, making them an excellent choice for maintaining a healthy weight and reducing fat in the liver.

### 5. Whole Fruits (Low in Sugar)

- **Examples**: Berries (blueberries, raspberries, strawberries), apples, pears, oranges, kiwis, and grapefruits.
- **Why They're Allowed**: These fruits are rich in antioxidants, fiber, and essential vitamins. Berries, in particular, are low in sugar and contain compounds that reduce liver inflammation and oxidative stress.

### 6. Healthy Fats (Unsaturated Fats)

- **Examples**: Olive oil, avocado, nuts (almonds, walnuts), and seeds (flaxseeds, chia seeds).
- **Why They're Allowed**: Unsaturated fats are heart-healthy and reduce liver inflammation. Olive oil, for instance, has been shown to improve liver enzyme levels and reduce fat buildup in the liver.

### 7. Herbal Teas and Coffee (Black)

- **Examples**: Green tea, dandelion tea, and plain black coffee.
- **Why They're Allowed**: Green tea contains catechins, which help reduce liver fat and inflammation. Coffee is rich in antioxidants and has been shown to lower the risk of liver fibrosis and fatty liver disease when consumed without sugar or cream.

### 8. Lean Animal Proteins

- **Examples**: Skinless chicken, turkey breast, and white fish (cod, haddock).
- **Why They're Allowed**: These proteins are low in saturated fats and help repair and build tissues without contributing to liver fat.

## 9. Spices and Herbs

- **Examples**: Turmeric, ginger, garlic, cinnamon, and parsley.
- **Why They're Allowed**: Spices like turmeric and garlic have anti-inflammatory and antioxidant properties that support liver health. They also enhance flavor without adding calories or sodium.

## 10. Water and Hydrating Beverages

- **Examples**: Plain water, sparkling water, herbal teas (unsweetened), and infused water with fruits or herbs.
- **Why They're Allowed**: Staying hydrated is essential for liver detoxification and overall health. Hydrating beverages also help prevent overeating and improve digestion.

## 11. Fermented Foods

- **Examples**: Kimchi, sauerkraut, kefir, and yogurt (unsweetened, low-fat).
- **Why They're Allowed**: Fermented foods support gut health by providing beneficial probiotics. A healthy gut microbiome is linked to reduced inflammation and better liver function.

## 12. Whole Grains (in Moderation)

- **Examples**: Brown rice, quinoa, farro, and whole-grain bread.
- **Why They're Allowed**: Whole grains provide essential nutrients like B vitamins and fiber, which improve digestion and help regulate blood sugar, reducing the risk of liver fat accumulation.

# RECIPES

If you have NAFLD, maintaining a healthy diet can be challenging. You need to make changes to your lifestyle, including your eating habits and exercise routine, and stick to them over time. We have chosen recipes that are both nutritious and delicious to help you meet the dietary requirements for NAFLD treatment. Our recipes and meal plans will help you increase your intake of total and prebiotic fiber, monounsaturated and polyunsaturated fats (including omega-3 fatty acids), and vitamin D, while also controlling your calorie intake to promote healthy weight loss. We have adapted simple recipes from a variety of North American cuisines using readily available **ingredients**. You can also use these recipes as a guide to adapt your own favorite recipes to the NAFLD diet.

Most of the dietary fiber we consume comes from fruits, vegetables, legumes, and whole grains. For example, prebiotic fiber helps reduce the amount of fat the liver can produce. Our meal plans and recipes include foods that are good sources of prebiotic fiber, such as garlic, leeks, onions, asparagus, wheat bran, whole wheat flour, and bananas.

The best sources of polyunsaturated fats are soft margarines made from sunflower, safflower, corn, and soybean oils. Omega-3 fatty acids are another type of polyunsaturated fat. Olive and canola oils, as well as soft margarines made from these oils, contain the highest amounts of monounsaturated fats.

Our recipes and meal plans emphasize eating fish and vegetable oils. We have included recipes for sardines, salmon, halibut, tuna, and cod to help improve the balance of omega-3 to omega-6 fatty acids in your diet.

It is important to consider not only the amount of fat you eat each day, but also the type of fat. Reduce your intake of saturated and trans fats by eating less animal products such as butter, meat, and full-fat dairy products. Also, limit processed foods. Saturated fats are found in animal products such as butter, meat, and full-fat dairy products, as well as other foods that contain fat. When preparing or cooking meals, choose monounsaturated and polyunsaturated fats over saturated and trans fats.

There are a few food sources that provide very small amounts of vitamin D. These include: salmon, tuna, sardines, orange juice, milk, yogurt, margarine, and eggs. Our meal plans and recipes include a variety of foods that are considered dietary sources of vitamin D.

**You can totally customize the recipes by swapping out ingredients—let your creativity run wild!**

# BREAKFAST

# OATMEAL WITH BERRIES AND NUTS

**SERVINGS**: 1

**DIFFICULTY**: Easy

**PREPARATION TIME**: 5 min.;
**COOKING TIME**: 10 min.

## INGREDIENTS:

- 1/2 cup rolled oats (40g)
- 1 cup water or milk (250ml)
- 1/2 cup berries (50g)
- 1/4 cup nuts (25g)

## INSTRUCTIONS:

1. Combine the oats and water or milk in a saucepan.
2. Bring to a boil, then reduce heat to low and simmer for 10 min..
3. Stir in the berries and nuts.

## NUTRITIONAL VALUES (per 100 gr.):

Calories: 140

Carbs: 25g

Protein: 5g

Fat: 5g

# YOGURT PARFAIT WITH FRUIT AND GRANOLA

**SERVINGS**: 1

**DIFFICULTY**: Easy

**PREPARATION TIME**: 5 min.

## INGREDIENTS:

- 1/2 cup yogurt (125g)
- 1/2 cup fruit, chopped (50g)
- 1/4 cup granola (25g)

## INSTRUCTIONS:

1. Layer the yogurt, fruit, and granola in a jar or glass.
2. Serve immediately.

## NUTRITIONAL VALUES (per 100 gr.):

Calories: 130

Carbs: 20g

Protein: 5g

Fat: 5g

# WHOLE-WHEAT TOAST WITH AVOCADO AND EGGS

**SERVINGS**: 1

**DIFFICULTY**: Easy

**PREPARATION TIME**: 5 min.;
**COOKING TIME**: 3 min.

## INGREDIENTS:

- 1 slice whole-wheat bread (30g)
- 1/4 avocado, mashed (15g)
- 1 egg (50g), cooked to your liking

## INSTRUCTIONS:

1. Toast the bread.
2. Spread the avocado on the toast.
3. Top with the cooked egg.
4. Serve immediately.

## NUTRITIONAL VALUES (per 100 gr.):

Calories: 200

Carbs: 15g

Protein: 10g

Fat: 10g

# SMOOTHIE WITH BERRIES, SPINACH, AND YOGURT

**SERVINGS**: 1

**DIFFICULTY**: Easy

**PREPARATION TIME**: 5 min.

## INGREDIENTS:

- 1 cup berries (100g)
- 1 handful of spinach (20g)
- 1/2 cup yogurt (125g)
- 1/2 cup milk or water (125ml)

## INSTRUCTIONS:

1. Combine all of the **ingredients** in a blender and blend until smooth and serve immediately

## NUTRITIONAL VALUES (per 100 gr.):

Calories: 90

Carbs: 15g

Protein: 5g

Fat: 1g

# CHIA PUDDING WITH BERRIES AND NUTS

**SERVINGS**: 1

**DIFFICULTY**: Easy

**PREPARATION TIME**: 10 min.;
Soaking time: overnight

## INGREDIENTS:

- 1/4 cup chia seeds (25g)
- 1 cup milk or water (250ml)
- 1/2 cup berries (50g)
- 1/4 cup nuts (25g)

## INSTRUCTIONS:

1. In a jar or bowl, combine the chia seeds and milk or water.

2. Stir well, then cover and refrigerate overnight.

3. In the morning, stir in the berries and nuts.

## NUTRITIONAL VALUES (per 100 gr.):

Calories: 140

Carbs: 15g

Protein: 5g

Fat: 5g

# WHOLE-WHEAT WAFFLES WITH PEANUT BUTTER AND BANANA

**SERVINGS**: 1

**DIFFICULTY**: Medium

**PREPARATION TIME**: 5 min.;
**COOKING TIME**: 5 min.

## INGREDIENTS:

- 1 whole-wheat waffle (100g)
- 1 tablespoon peanut butter (15g)
- 1/2 banana (50g), sliced

## INSTRUCTIONS:

1. Toast the waffle.
2. Spread the peanut butter on the waffle.
3. Top with the banana slices.
4. Serve immediately.

## NUTRITIONAL VALUES (per 100 gr.):

Calories: 200

Carbs: 25g

Protein: 10g

Fat: 10g

## OATMEAL WITH PEANUT BUTTER AND CHIA SEEDS

**SERVINGS**: 1

**DIFFICULTY**: Easy

**PREPARATION TIME**: 5 min.;
**COOKING TIME**: 10 min.

### INGREDIENTS:

- 1/2 cup rolled oats (40g)
- 1 cup water or milk (250ml)
- 1 tablespoon peanut butter (15g)
- 1 tablespoon chia seeds (10g)

### INSTRUCTIONS:

1. Combine the oats, water or milk, peanut butter, and chia seeds in a saucepan.

2. Bring to a boil, then reduce heat to low and simmer for 10 min., or until the oats are cooked through.

### NUTRITIONAL VALUES (per 100 gr.):

Calories: 140

Carbs: 20g

Protein: 5g

Fat: 5g


## SCRAMBLED EGGS WITH VEGETABLES

**SERVINGS**: 1

**DIFFICULTY**: Easy

**PREPARATION TIME**: 5 min.;
**COOKING TIME**: 5 min.

### INGREDIENTS:

- 2 eggs (100g)
- 1/4 cup vegetables, chopped, such as onions, peppers, or mushrooms (25g)
- Salt and pepper to taste

### INSTRUCTIONS:

1. Whisk the eggs in a bowl.
2. Add the vegetables and salt and pepper to taste.
3. Heat a small skillet over medium heat.
4. Add the egg mixture to the skillet and cook until scrambled to your liking.
5. Serve immediately.

### NUTRITIONAL VALUES (per 100 gr.):

Calories: 130

Carbs: 1g

Protein: 15g

Fat: 7g

# YOGURT PARFAIT WITH GRANOLA AND NUTS

**SERVINGS**: 1

**DIFFICULTY**: Easy

**PREPARATION TIME**: 5 min.

## INGREDIENTS:

- 1/2 cup yogurt (125g)
- 1/4 cup granola (25g)
- 1/4 cup nuts (25g)

## INSTRUCTIONS:

1. Layer the yogurt, granola, and nuts in a jar or glass.

2. Serve immediately.

## NUTRITIONAL VALUES (per 100 gr.):

Calories: 130

Carbs: 20g

Protein: 5g

Fat: 5g

# SMOOTHIE WITH BERRIES, SPINACH, AND ALMOND BUTTER

**SERVINGS**: 1

**DIFFICULTY**: Easy

**PREPARATION TIME**: 5 min.

## INGREDIENTS:

- 1 cup berries (100g)
- 1 handful of spinach (20g)
- 1/2 cup almond butter (60g)
- 1/2 cup milk or water (125ml)

## INSTRUCTIONS:

1. Combine all of the **ingredients** in a blender and blend until smooth.
2. Serve immediately.

## NUTRITIONAL VALUES (per 100 gr.):

Calories: 150

Carbs: 15g

Protein: 5g

Fat: 10g

## WHOLE-WHEAT TOAST WITH AVOCADO AND TOMATOES

**SERVINGS**: 1

**DIFFICULTY**: Easy

**PREPARATION TIME**: 5 min.

### INGREDIENTS:

- 1 slice whole-wheat bread (30g)
- 1/4 avocado, mashed (15g)
- 1/2 tomato (50g), sliced

### INSTRUCTIONS:

1. Toast the bread.
2. Spread the avocado on the toast.
3. Top with the tomato slices.
4. Serve immediately.

### NUTRITIONAL VALUES (per 100 gr.):

Calories: 150

Carbs: 20g

Protein: 5g

Fat: 5g

## HARD-BOILED EGGS WITH FRUIT AND NUTS

**SERVINGS**: 1

**DIFFICULTY**: Easy

**PREPARATION TIME**: 10 min.;
**COOKING TIME**: 10 min.

### INGREDIENTS:

- 2 eggs (100g)
- 1/2 cup fruit, chopped (50g)
- 1/4 cup nuts (25g)

### INSTRUCTIONS:

1. Place the eggs in a single layer in a saucepan and cover with cold water.
2. Bring the water to a boil over high heat.
3. Once the water is boiling, cover the saucepan and remove it from the heat.
4. Let the eggs stand in the hot water for 10 min..
5. Drain the hot water and run cold water over the eggs until they are cool to the touch.
6. Peel the eggs and serve them with fruit and nuts.

### NUTRITIONAL VALUES (per 100 gr.):

Calories: 140

Carbs: 1g

Protein: 15g

Fat: 7g

# COTTAGE CHEESE WITH BERRIES AND NUTS

**SERVINGS**: 1

**DIFFICULTY**: Easy

**PREPARATION TIME**: 5 min.

## INGREDIENTS:

- 1/2 cup cottage cheese (125g)
- 1/2 cup berries (50g)
- 1/4 cup nuts (25g)

## INSTRUCTIONS:

1. In a bowl, combine the cottage cheese, berries, and nuts.
2. Serve immediately.

## NUTRITIONAL VALUES (per 100 gr.):

Calories: 120

Carbs: 10g

Protein: 15g

Fat: 2g

# SMOOTHIE WITH AVOCADO, BANANA, AND SPINACH

**SERVINGS**: 1

**DIFFICULTY**: Easy

**PREPARATION TIME**: 5 min.

## INGREDIENTS:

- 1/2 avocado (75g)
- 1 banana (100g)
- 1 handful of spinach (20g)
- 1 cup milk or water (250ml)

## INSTRUCTIONS:

1. Combine all of the **ingredients** in a blender and blend until smooth.
2. Serve immediately.

## NUTRITIONAL VALUES (per 100 gr.):

Calories: 140

Carbs: 15g

Protein: 5g

Fat: 7g

## WHOLE-WHEAT PANCAKES WITH APPLES AND CINNAMON

**SERVINGS**: 1

**DIFFICULTY**: Easy

**PREPARATION TIME**: 5 min.;
**COOKING TIME**: 10 min.

### INGREDIENTS:

- 1/2 cup whole-wheat flour (60g)
- 1/4 teaspoon baking powder (1.25g)
- 1/4 teaspoon baking soda (1.25g)
- 1/4 teaspoon salt (1.25g)
- 1/4 teaspoon cinnamon (1.25g)
- 1/2 cup milk (125ml)
- 1 egg (50g)
- 1/4 cup applesauce (60g)
- 1/4 cup chopped apple (30g)

### INSTRUCTIONS:

1. In a bowl, whisk together the flour, baking powder, baking soda, salt, and cinnamon.

2. In a separate bowl, whisk together the milk, egg, applesauce, and chopped apple.

3. Add the wet **ingredients** to the dry **ingredients** and whisk until just combined.

4. Heat a small skillet over medium heat. Grease the skillet with a little cooking spray.

5. Pour 1/4 cup of batter onto the skillet for each pancake. Cook for 2-3 min. per side, or until golden brown.

6. Serve immediately with your favorite toppings, such as maple syrup, honey, or fresh fruit.

**NUTRITIONAL VALUES** (per 100 gr.):

Calories: 150

Carbs: 25g

Protein: 5g

Fat: 5g

~~~~~~~~~~~~~~~~

## QUINOA PORRIDGE WITH BERRIES AND NUTS

**SERVINGS**: 1

**DIFFICULTY**: Easy

**PREPARATION TIME**: 5 min.;
**COOKING TIME**: 15 min.

### INGREDIENTS:

- 1/4 cup quinoa (30g)
- 1 cup milk or water (250ml)
- 1/4 teaspoon salt (1.25g)
- 1/2 cup berries (50g)
- 1/4 cup nuts (25g)

**NUTRITIONAL VALUES** (per 100 gr.):

Calories: 150

Carbs: 25g

Protein: 5g

Fat: 5g

### INSTRUCTIONS:

1. In a saucepan, combine the quinoa, milk or water, and salt.

2. Bring to a boil over medium heat.

3. Reduce heat to low and simmer for 15 min., or until the quinoa is cooked through.

4. Stir in the berries and nuts.

5. Serve immediately.

~~~~~~~~~

# SMOOTHIE WITH SPINACH, KALE, AND BANANA

**SERVINGS**: 1

**DIFFICULTY**: Easy

**PREPARATION TIME**: 5 min.

**INGREDIENTS**:

- 1 handful of spinach (20g)
- 1 handful of kale (20g)
- 1 banana (100g)
- 1 cup milk or water (250ml)

**INSTRUCTIONS**:

1. Combine all of the **INGREDIENTS** in a blender and blend until smooth.

2. Serve immediately.

**NUTRITIONAL VALUES** (per 100 gr.):

Calories: 100

Carbs: 20g

Protein: 3g

Fat: 1g

# OATMEAL WITH BERRIES AND YOGURT

**SERVINGS**: 1

**DIFFICULTY**: Easy

**PREPARATION TIME**: 5 min.;
**COOKING TIME**: 10 min.

**INGREDIENTS**:

- 1/2 cup rolled oats (40g)
- 1 cup water or milk (250ml)
- 1/4 cup berries (50g)
- 1/4 cup yogurt (60g)

**INSTRUCTIONS**:

1. Combine the oats and water or milk in a saucepan.

2. Bring to a boil, then reduce heat to low and simmer for 10 min..

3. Stir in the berries and yogurt.

**NUTRITIONAL VALUES** (per 100 gr.):

Calories: 150

Carbs: 25g

Protein: 5g

Fat: 5g

# SMOOTHIE WITH AVOCADO, BANANA, AND BERRIES

**SERVINGS**: 1

**DIFFICULTY**: Easy

**PREPARATION TIME**: 5 min.

## INGREDIENTS:

- 1/2 avocado (75g)
- 1 banana (100g)
- 1/2 cup berries (50g)
- 1 cup milk or water (250ml)

## INSTRUCTIONS:

1. Combine all of the **ingredients** in a blender and blend until smooth. Serve immediately.

## NUTRITIONAL VALUES (per 100 gr.):

Calories: 150

Carbs: 25g

Protein: 5g

Fat: 7g

# MAIN MEAL

# GRILLED SALMON WITH ROASTED VEGETABLES

**SERVINGS**: 1

**DIFFICULTY**: Easy

**PREPARATION TIME**: 10 min.;
**COOKING TIME**: 20 min.

## INGREDIENTS:

- 1 (6-ounce) salmon fillet (170g)

- 1 tablespoon olive oil (15ml)

- 1/2 teaspoon salt (2.5g)

- 1/4 teaspoon black pepper (1.25g)

- 1 cup chopped vegetables, such as broccoli, carrots, and potatoes (100g)

## INSTRUCTIONS:

1. Preheat oven to 400 degrees F (200 degrees C).

2. Brush the salmon fillet with olive oil and season with salt and pepper.

3. Place the salmon fillet on a baking sheet lined with parchment paper.

4. Roast the salmon for 15-20 min., or until cooked through.

5. While the salmon is roasting, toss the vegetables with olive oil, salt, and pepper.

6. Spread the vegetables on a baking sheet lined with parchment paper.

7. Roast the vegetables for 20-25 min., or until tender.

8. Serve the salmon with the roasted vegetables.

**NUTRITIONAL VALUES** (per 100 gr.):

Calories: 200

Carbs: 10g

Protein: 30g

Fat: 10g

~~~~~~~~~~

# LENTIL SOUP

**SERVINGS**: 1

**DIFFICULTY**: Easy

**PREPARATION TIME**: 10 min.;
**COOKING TIME**: 30 min.

## INGREDIENTS:

- 1 cup lentils (200g)

- 2 cups vegetable broth (500ml)

- 1/2 cup chopped onion (50g)

- 1/4 cup chopped carrot (25g)

- 1/4 cup chopped celery (25g)

- 1 teaspoon garlic powder (5g)

- 1/2 teaspoon dried oregano (2.5g)

- 1/4 teaspoon salt (1.25g)

- 1/4 teaspoon black pepper (1.25g)

## INSTRUCTIONS:

1. In a large saucepan, combine the lentils, vegetable broth, onion, carrot, celery, garlic powder, oregano, salt, and pepper.

2. Bring to a boil over medium heat.

3. Reduce heat to low and simmer for 30 min., or until the lentils are tender.

4. Serve the soup hot.

**NUTRITIONAL VALUES** (per 100 gr.):

Calories: 150

Carbs: 25g

Protein: 10g

Fat: 5g

〜〜〜〜〜〜〜

# QUINOA SALAD WITH ROASTED VEGETABLES AND CHICKPEAS

**SERVINGS**: 1

**DIFFICULTY**: Easy

**PREPARATION TIME**: 10 min.;
**COOKING TIME**: 30 min.

**INGREDIENTS**:

- 1 cup cooked quinoa (100g)

- 1 cup chopped roasted vegetables, such as broccoli, carrots, and potatoes (100g)

- 1/2 cup cooked chickpeas (100g)

- 1 tablespoon olive oil (15ml)

- 1 tablespoon lemon juice (15ml)

- 1/4 teaspoon salt (1.25g)

- 1/4 teaspoon black pepper (1.25g)

**INSTRUCTIONS**:

1. In a large bowl, combine the quinoa, roasted vegetables, chickpeas, olive oil, lemon juice, salt, and pepper.

2. Toss to combine.

3. Serve the salad hot or cold.

**NUTRITIONAL VALUES** (per 100 gr.):

Calories: 200

Carbs: 25g

Protein: 10g

Fat: 10g

〜〜〜〜〜〜〜

# LENTIL AND VEGETABLE CURRY

**SERVINGS**: 1

**DIFFICULTY**: Easy

**PREPARATION TIME**: 10 min.;
**COOKING TIME**: 30 min.

**INGREDIENTS**:

- 1 tablespoon olive oil (15ml)

- 1/2 cup chopped onion (50g)

- 1 teaspoon garlic powder (5g)

- 1 teaspoon curry powder (5g)

- 1/2 teaspoon ground cumin (2.5g)

- 1/4 teaspoon salt (1.25g)

- 1/4 teaspoon black pepper (1.25g)

- 1 cup lentils (200g)

- 1 cup vegetable broth (250ml)

- 1 cup chopped vegetables, such as carrots, potatoes, and broccoli (100g)

**INSTRUCTIONS**:

1. Heat the olive oil in a large saucepan over medium heat.

2. Add the onion and cook until softened, about 5 min..

3. Add the garlic powder, curry powder, cumin, salt, and pepper and cook for 1 minute more.

4. Add the lentils, vegetable broth, and vegetables to the saucepan.

5. Bring to a boil, then reduce heat to low and simmer for 20 min., or until the lentils are tender.

6. Serve the curry hot.

## NUTRITIONAL VALUES (per 100 gr.):

Calories: 150

Carbs: 25g

Protein: 10g

Fat: 5g

~~~~~~~~~~~~~~~~~~~~

# TOFU SCRAMBLE WITH VEGETABLES

**SERVINGS**: 1

**DIFFICULTY**: Easy

**PREPARATION TIME**: 5 min.;
**COOKING TIME**: 10 min.

## INGREDIENTS:

- 1 tablespoon olive oil (15ml)

- 1/2 block extra firm tofu, crumbled (150g)

- 1/2 cup chopped vegetables, such as onions, peppers, and mushrooms (50g)

- 1/4 cup chopped tomato (25g)

- 1/4 teaspoon salt (1.25g)

- 1/4 teaspoon black pepper (1.25g)

## INSTRUCTIONS:

1. Heat the olive oil in a small skillet over medium heat.

2. Add the tofu scramble and vegetables to the skillet and cook until the vegetables are tender and the tofu is heated through, about 10 min..

3. Season with salt and pepper to taste.

4. Serve immediately.

## NUTRITIONAL VALUES (per 100 gr.):

Calories: 150

Carbs: 10g

Protein: 15g

Fat: 7g

~~~~~~~~~~~~~~~~~~~~

# CHICKEN AND VEGETABLE STIR-FRY

**SERVINGS**: 1

**DIFFICULTY**: Easy

**PREPARATION TIME**: 10 min.;
**COOKING TIME**: 15 min.

## INGREDIENTS:

- 1 tablespoon olive oil (15ml)

- 1/2 pound boneless, skinless chicken breast, cut into bite-sized pieces (225g)

- 1 cup chopped vegetables, such as onions, peppers, and broccoli (100g)

- 1/4 cup soy sauce (60ml)

- 1 tablespoon cornstarch (10g)

- 1/4 teaspoon ground ginger (1.25g)

- 1/4 teaspoon garlic powder (1.25g)

- 1/4 teaspoon salt (1.25g)
- 1/4 teaspoon black pepper (1.25g)

## INSTRUCTIONS:

1. In a small bowl, combine the soy sauce, cornstarch, ginger, garlic powder, salt, and pepper.

2. Add the chicken to the soy sauce mixture and toss to coat.

3. Heat the olive oil in a large skillet or wok over medium-high heat.

4. Add the chicken to the skillet and cook until browned on all sides.

5. Add the vegetables to the skillet and cook until tender, about 5 min..

6. Add the soy sauce mixture to the skillet and cook until the sauce has thickened, about 1 minute.

7. Serve immediately.

## NUTRITIONAL VALUES (per 100 gr.):

Calories: 150

Carbs: 10g

Protein: 20g

Fat: 5g

# TURKEY MEATBALLS WITH SPAGHETTI SQUASH

**SERVINGS**: 1

**DIFFICULTY**: Easy

**PREPARATION TIME**: 15 min.;
**COOKING TIME**: 30 min.

## INGREDIENTS:

- 1 pound ground turkey (450g)

- 1/2 cup chopped onion (50g)

- 1/4 cup bread crumbs (25g)

- 1/4 cup grated Parmesan cheese (25g)

- 1 egg (50g)

- 1/4 cup chopped parsley (25g)

- 1 teaspoon garlic powder (5g)

- 1/2 teaspoon dried oregano (2.5g)

- 1/4 teaspoon salt (1.25g)

- 1/4 teaspoon black pepper (1.25g)

- 1 spaghetti squash (1.5kg)

## INSTRUCTIONS:

1. Preheat oven to 200 degrees F

2. In a large bowl, combine the turkey, onion, bread crumbs, Parmesan cheese, egg, parsley, garlic powder, oregano, salt, and pepper.

3. Mix well.

4. Form the turkey mixture into meatballs, about 1 inch in diameter.

5. Place the meatballs on a baking sheet lined with parchment paper.

6. Bake the meatballs for 20 min., or until cooked through.

7. While the meatballs are baking, cut the spaghetti squash in half lengthwise and remove the seeds.

8. Place the spaghetti squash halves face down on a baking sheet lined with parchment paper.

9. Bake the spaghetti squash for 45-60 min., or until tender.

10. Once the spaghetti squash is tender, use a fork to scrape the flesh into strands.

11. Serve the turkey meatballs with the spaghetti squash.

## NUTRITIONAL VALUES (per 100 gr.):

Calories: 150

Carbs: 10g

Protein: 20g

Fat: 5g

~~~~~~~~~~~~~~

# GRILLED SHRIMP WITH ROASTED VEGETABLES

**SERVINGS**: 1

**DIFFICULTY**: Easy

**PREPARATION TIME**: 10 min.;
**COOKING TIME**: 20 min.

## INGREDIENTS:

- 1 pound shrimp, peeled and deveined (450g)
- 1 tablespoon olive oil (15ml)
- 1/2 teaspoon salt (2.5g)
- 1/4 teaspoon black pepper (1.25g)
- 1 cup chopped vegetables, such as broccoli, carrots, and potatoes (100g)

## INSTRUCTIONS:

1. Preheat grill to medium heat.
2. Brush the shrimp with olive oil and season with salt and pepper.
3. Grill the shrimp for 2-3 min. per side, or until cooked through.
4. While the shrimp is grilling, toss the vegetables with olive oil, salt, and pepper.
5. Grill the vegetables for 5-10 min., or until tender.
6. Serve the grilled shrimp with the roasted vegetables.

## NUTRITIONAL VALUES (per 100 gr.):

Calories: 150

Carbs: 10g

Protein: 20g

Fat: 5g

~~~~~~~~~~~~~~

# TUNA AND WALNUT SALAD

**SERVINGS**: 4

**DIFFICULTY**: Easy

**PREPARATION TIME**: 15 minutes

**COOKING TIME**: Not applicable (uses canned tuna)

## INGREDIENTS:

- 2 (5 oz) cans tuna packed in water, drained and flaked
- 1/2 cup chopped celery
- 1/4 cup chopped red onion
- 1/4 cup chopped walnuts
- 2 tablespoons mayonnaise (or Greek yogurt for a lighter option)
- 1 tablespoon lemon juice
- 1/4 teaspoon dried dill (or other fresh herbs like parsley or chives)
- Salt and freshly ground black pepper, to taste

## INSTRUCTIONS:

1. In a medium bowl, combine flaked tuna, chopped celery, red onion, and walnuts.
2. In a separate bowl, whisk together mayonnaise, lemon juice, dill, salt, and pepper.
3. Add the dressing to the tuna mixture and toss to coat evenly.
4. Taste and adjust seasonings as needed.
5. Serve the tuna and walnut salad on a bed of lettuce, with crackers, or on bread as a sandwich filling.

## NUTRITIONAL VALUES (per serving - approximate):

Calories: 300

Carbs: 10g

Protein: 25g

Fat: 15g

~~~~~~~~~~~~~~~~

# QUINOA SALAD WITH CHICKPEAS AND AVOCADO

**SERVINGS**: 1

**DIFFICULTY**: Easy

**PREPARATION TIME**: 10 min.;
**COOKING TIME**: 15 min.

## INGREDIENTS:

- 1 cup cooked quinoa (100g)
- 1/2 cup cooked chickpeas (100g)
- 1/2 avocado, sliced (50g)
- 1/4 cup chopped red onion (25g)
- 1/4 cup chopped cucumber (25g)
- 1 tablespoon olive oil (15ml)
- 1 tablespoon lemon juice (15ml)
- 1/4 teaspoon salt (1.25g)
- 1/4 teaspoon black pepper (1.25g)

## INSTRUCTIONS:

1. In a large bowl, combine the quinoa, chickpeas, avocado, red onion, and cucumber.
2. In a small bowl, whisk together the olive oil, lemon juice, salt, and pepper.
3. Pour the dressing over the quinoa salad and toss to combine.
4. Serve immediately.

## NUTRITIONAL VALUES (per 100 gr.):

Calories: 150

Carbs: 10g

Protein: 15g

Fat: 7g

~~~~~~~~~~~~~~~~

# BLACK BEAN BURGERS WITH SWEET POTATO FRIES

**SERVINGS**: 1

**DIFFICULTY**: Easy

**PREPARATION TIME**: 20 min.;
**COOKING TIME**: 30 min.

## INGREDIENTS:

- 1 (15-ounce) can black beans, rinsed and drained (425g)
- 1/2 cup cooked brown rice (100g)
- 1/4 cup chopped onion (25g)
- 1/4 cup chopped bell pepper (25g)
- 1/4 teaspoon garlic powder (1.25g)
- 1/4 teaspoon chili powder (1.25g)
- 1/4 teaspoon salt (1.25g)
- 1/4 teaspoon black pepper (1.25g)
- 1 sweet potato, peeled and sliced (300g)
- 1 tablespoon olive oil (15ml)

- **INSTRUCTIONS**:

- Preheat oven to 400 degrees F (200 degrees C).

- In a food processor, combine the black beans, brown rice, onion, bell pepper, garlic powder, chili powder, salt, and pepper.

- Pulse until the mixture is well combined.

- Form the mixture into patties.

- Place the patties on a baking sheet lined with parchment paper.

- Bake the patties for 20 min., or until cooked through.

- While the patties are baking, toss the sweet potato slices with olive oil, salt, and pepper.

## NUTRITIONAL VALUES (per 100 gr.):

Calories: 200

Carbs: 25g

Protein: 10g

Fat: 10g

~~~~~~~~~~~

# LENTIL AND VEGETABLE SOUP WITH WHOLE-WHEAT BREAD

**SERVINGS**: 1

**DIFFICULTY**: Easy

**PREPARATION TIME**: 10 min.;
**COOKING TIME**: 30 min.

## INGREDIENTS:

- 1 cup lentils (200g)

- 2 cups vegetable broth (500ml)

- 1/2 cup chopped onion (50g)

- 1/4 cup chopped carrot (25g)

- 1/4 cup chopped celery (25g)

- 1 teaspoon garlic powder (5g)

- 1/2 teaspoon dried oregano (2.5g)

- 1/4 teaspoon salt (1.25g)

- 1/4 teaspoon black pepper (1.25g)

- 1 slice whole-wheat bread (25g)

## INSTRUCTIONS:

1. In a large saucepan, combine the lentils, vegetable broth, onion, carrot, celery, garlic powder, oregano, salt, and pepper.

2. Bring to a boil over medium heat.

3. Reduce heat to low and simmer for 20 min., or until the lentils are tender.

4. Serve the soup with a slice of whole-wheat bread.

## NUTRITIONAL VALUES (per 100 gr.):

Calories: 150

Carbs: 25g

Protein: 10g

Fat: 5g

# TUNA STEAKS WITH AVOCADO

**SERVINGS**: 2

**DIFFICULTY**: Easy

**PREPARATION TIME**: 10 minutes;

**COOKING TIME**: (depending on desired doneness)

## INGREDIENTS:

- 2 tuna steaks (each about 6 ounces)
- 1 tablespoon olive oil
- Salt and freshly ground black pepper, to taste
- 1 ripe avocado, sliced
- Lemon wedges, for garnish (optional)

## INSTRUCTIONS:

1. Pat the tuna steaks dry with paper towels. Season generously with salt and pepper.
2. Heat olive oil in a large skillet over medium-high heat. Sear the tuna steaks for 2-3 minutes per side for a rare sear, or longer for a more well-done finish.
3. While the tuna cooks, slice the avocado.
4. Once cooked to your preference, remove the tuna from the pan and let it rest for a few minutes before serving.
5. Plate the tuna steaks and top with sliced avocado.
6. Garnish with lemon wedges (optional) and serve immediately.

## NUTRITIONAL VALUES (per serving):

Calories: 400

Carbs: 5g

Protein: 50g

Fat: 25g

# SPICY GINGER CHICKEN

**SERVINGS**: 2

**DIFFICULTY**: Easy

**PREPARATION TIME**: 10 minutes

**COOKING TIME**: 15-20 minutes

## INGREDIENTS:

- 1 tablespoon olive oil
- 1/2 pound boneless, skinless chicken breast, cut into bite-sized pieces
- 1/2 cup chopped vegetables (such as bell peppers, onions, or broccoli)
- 1-2 tablespoons soy sauce
- 1 tablespoon cornstarch
- 1-2 teaspoons grated ginger (depending on desired spice level)
- 1/2 teaspoon red pepper flakes (adjust for spice preference)
- 1 clove garlic, minced
- Salt and freshly ground black pepper, to taste
- Cooked rice or noodles (optional)

## INSTRUCTIONS:

1. Heat olive oil in a large skillet or wok over medium-high heat.
2. Add chicken pieces and cook for 5-7 minutes, or until golden brown and cooked through.
3. Remove chicken from the pan and set aside.
4. Add chopped vegetables to the pan and cook for 2-3 minutes, or until tender-crisp.
5. In a small bowl, whisk together soy sauce, cornstarch, ginger, red pepper flakes, and garlic. (Start with 1 teaspoon of ginger and red pepper flakes, then adjust to your spice preference).
6. Pour the sauce mixture into the pan with the vegetables and bring to a simmer.
7. Add the cooked chicken back to the pan and toss to coat with the sauce.
8. Season with salt and pepper to taste.
   Serve the spicy ginger chicken over cooked rice or noodles (optional).

## NUTRITIONAL VALUES (per serving - approximate):

Calories: 300 - 400

Carbs: 40g

Protein: 35g

Fat: 18g

# SHRIMP AND BROCCOLI STIR FRY

**SERVINGS**: 2

**DIFFICULTY**: Easy

**PREPARATION TIME:** 10 minutes

**COOKING TIME**: 10-12 minutes

INGREDIENTS:

- 1 tablespoon olive oil
- 1/2 pound medium shrimp, peeled and deveined
- 1 cup broccoli florets
- 1/2 cup chopped red bell pepper (optional)
- 1/4 cup chopped onion (optional)
- 2 cloves garlic, minced
- 1 tablespoon soy sauce
- 1 tablespoon cornstarch
- 1/4 cup water or chicken broth
- 1 teaspoon sesame oil (optional)
- Salt and freshly ground black pepper, to taste
- Cooked rice or noodles (optional)

INSTRUCTIONS:

1. Heat olive oil in a large skillet or wok over medium-high heat.
2. Add shrimp and cook for 2-3 minutes per side, or until pink and opaque. Remove shrimp from the pan and set aside.
3. Add broccoli florets (and optional bell pepper and onion) to the pan and cook for 3-4 minutes, or until tender-crisp.

In a small bowl, whisk together soy sauce, cornstarch, water or chicken broth, and sesame oil (if using).

Pour the sauce mixture into the pan with the vegetables and bring to a simmer.

Add the cooked shrimp back to the pan and toss to coat with the sauce.

Season with salt and pepper to taste.

Serve the shrimp and broccoli stir fry over cooked rice or noodles (optional).

NUTRITIONAL VALUES (per serving - approximate):

Calories: 300-350

Carbs: 20-30g (depending on whether or not you serve it with rice or noodles)

Protein: 30-35g

Fat: 10-15g

# SIDE DISHES

# CHICKEN AND BROWN RICE STIR-FRY

**SERVINGS**: 1

**DIFFICULTY**: Easy

**PREPARATION TIME**: 10 min.;
**COOKING TIME**: 15 min.

## INGREDIENTS:

- 1 tablespoon olive oil (15ml)
- 1/2 pound boneless, skinless chicken breast, cut into bite-sized pieces (225g)
- 1 cup chopped vegetables, such as onions, peppers, and broccoli (100g)
- 1/4 cup soy sauce (60ml)
- 1 tablespoon cornstarch (10g)
- 1/4 teaspoon ground ginger (1.25g)
- 1/4 teaspoon garlic powder (1.25g)
- 1/4 teaspoon salt (1.25g)
- 1/4 teaspoon black pepper (1.25g)
- 1/2 cup cooked brown rice (100g)

## INSTRUCTIONS:

1. In a small bowl, combine the soy sauce, cornstarch, ginger, garlic powder, salt, and pepper.
2. Add the chicken to the soy sauce mixture and toss to coat.
3. Heat the olive oil in a large skillet or wok over medium-high heat.
4. Add the chicken to the skillet and cook until browned on all sides.
5. Add the vegetables to the skillet and cook until tender, about 5 min..
6. Add the soy sauce mixture to the skillet and cook until the sauce has thickened, about 1 minute.

Serve the chicken and vegetable stir-fry over cooked brown rice.

## NUTRITIONAL VALUES (per 100 gr.):

Calories: 150

Carbs: 25g

Protein: 20g

Fat: 5g

# ROASTED CARROTS

**SERVINGS**: 1

**DIFFICULTY**: Easy

**PREPARATION TIME**: 10 min.;
**COOKING TIME**: 25 min.

## INGREDIENTS:

- 1 cup carrots, peeled and sliced (100g)
- 1 tablespoon olive oil (15ml)
- 1/4 teaspoon salt (1.25g)
- 1/4 teaspoon black pepper (1.25g)

## INSTRUCTIONS:

1. Preheat oven to 400 degrees F (200 degrees C).
2. Peel and slice the carrots.
3. Toss the carrots with olive oil, salt, and pepper.
4. Spread the carrots on a baking sheet and roast for 20-25 minutes, or until tender and golden brown.
5. Enjoy!

**NUTRITIONAL VALUES** (per 100 gr.):

Calories: 50

Carbs: 10g

Protein: 1g

Fat: 1.5g

~~~~~~~~~~~~~~~~~~~~

# STEAMED GREEN BEANS

**SERVINGS**: 1

**DIFFICULTY**: Medium

**PREPARATION TIME**: 5 min.;
**COOKING TIME**: 10 min.

**INGREDIENTS**:

- 1 cup green beans, trimmed (100g)

**NUTRITIONAL VALUES** (per 100 gr.):

Calories: 30

Carbs: 7g

Protein: 2g

Fat: 0.5g

**INSTRUCTIONS**

1. Wash the green beans and trim the ends.
2. Bring a pot of water to a boil.
3. Add the green beans to the boiling water and cook for 5-7 minutes, or until they are bright green and tender.
4. Drain the green beans and season with salt and pepper to taste.

# ROASTED ZUCCHINI

**SERVINGS**: 1

**DIFFICULTY**: Easy

**PREPARATION TIME**: 10 min.;
**COOKING TIME**: 20 min.

**INGREDIENTS**:

- 1 zucchini, sliced (100g)
- 1 tablespoon olive oil (15ml)
- 1/4 teaspoon salt (1.25g)
- 1/4 teaspoon black pepper (1.25g)

**NUTRITIONAL VALUES** (per 100 gr.):

Calories: 20

Carbs: 4g

Protein: 1.5g

Fat: 0.5g

**INSTRUCTIONS**:

1. Preheat the oven to 400 degrees Fahrenheit (200 degrees Celsius).
2. Cut the zucchini into 1/2-inch thick slices.
3. Toss the zucchini slices with olive oil, salt, and pepper.
4. Spread the zucchini slices on a baking sheet and bake for 20-25 minutes, or until the zucchini is tender and golden brown.

# MASHED CAULIFLOWER

**SERVINGS**: 1

**DIFFICULTY**: Easy

**PREPARATION TIME**: 10 min.;
**COOKING TIME**: 15 min.

## INGREDIENTS:

- 1 head of cauliflower, cut into florets (400g)
- 1/4 cup milk (60ml)
- 1 tablespoon butter (15g)
- 1/4 teaspoon salt (1.25g)
- 1/4 teaspoon black pepper (1.25g)

## NUTRITIONAL VALUES (per 100 gr.):

Calories: 50

Carbs: 6g

Protein: 2g

Fat: 3g

## INSTRUCTIONS:

1. In a large pot, bring a pot of salted water to a boil.

2. Add the cauliflower florets to the boiling water and cook for 10 min., or until tender.

3. Drain the cauliflower florets and return them to the pot.

4. Add the milk, butter, salt, and pepper to the cauliflower florets and mash until smooth.

# ROASTED TOMATOES

**SERVINGS**: 1

**DIFFICULTY**: Easy

**PREPARATION TIME**: 10 min.;
**COOKING TIME**: 20 min.

## INGREDIENTS:

- 1 cup cherry tomatoes, halved (100g)
- 1 tablespoon olive oil (15ml)
- 1/4 teaspoon salt (1.25g)
- 1/4 teaspoon black pepper (1.25g)

## INSTRUCTIONS:

1. Preheat the oven to 400 degrees Fahrenheit (200 degrees Celsius)

2. Cut the tomatoes into halves or quarters.

3. Toss the tomato halves or quarters with olive oil, salt, and pepper.

4. Spread the tomato halves or quarters on a baking sheet and bake for 20-25 minutes, or until the tomatoes are soft and slightly caramelized.

## NUTRITIONAL VALUES (per 100 gr.):

Calories: 30

Carbs: 5g

Protein: 1g

Fat: 1.5g

# ROASTED RED PEPPERS

**SERVINGS**: 1

**DIFFICULTY**: Easy

**PREPARATION TIME**: 10 min.;
**COOKING TIME**: 20 min.

## INGREDIENTS:

1 red pepper, sliced (100g)

1 tablespoon olive oil (15ml)

1/4 teaspoon black pepper (1.25g)

## INSTRUCTIONS:

1. Preheat the oven to 400 degrees Fahrenheit (200 degrees Celsius).

2. Cut the red peppers in half and remove the seeds.

3. Place the red peppers on a baking sheet and drizzle with olive oil.

4. Roast the red peppers in the preheated oven for 20-25 minutes, or until the peppers are soft and slightly charred.

## NUTRITIONAL VALUES (per 100 gr.):

Calories: 30

Carbs: 5g

Protein: 1g

Fat: 1.5g

# MEDITERRANEAN TOMATO BASIL SAUCE

**SERVINGS**: 4-6

**DIFFICULTY**: Easy

**PREPARATION TIME**: 10 minutes

**COOKING TIME**: 30-40 minutes

## INGREDIENTS:

- 2 tablespoons olive oil
- 1 medium onion, finely chopped
- 2 cloves garlic, minced
- 1 (28-ounce) can crushed tomatoes
- 1 (14.5-ounce) can diced tomatoes, undrained
- 1/2 cup vegetable broth (or water)
- 1 tablespoon tomato paste
- 1/2 teaspoon dried oregano
- 1/4 teaspoon dried thyme
- Salt and freshly ground black pepper, to taste
- 1/4 cup fresh basil leaves, chopped (plus extra for garnish)

## INSTRUCTIONS:

1. Heat olive oil in a large saucepan over medium heat. Add chopped onion and cook for 5-7 minutes, or until softened and translucent.
2. Add minced garlic and cook for an additional minute, until fragrant.
3. Stir in crushed tomatoes, diced tomatoes with their juices, vegetable broth, tomato paste, oregano, and thyme.
4. Season with salt and pepper to taste.
5. Bring the sauce to a simmer, then reduce heat to low and let it simmer for 30-40 minutes, stirring occasionally. This allows the flavors to develop and the sauce to thicken.
6. While the sauce is simmering, chop the fresh basil leaves.
7. Once the sauce has reached your desired consistency, remove it from the heat.
8. Stir in the chopped basil leaves (reserve some for garnish).
9. Adjust seasonings with salt and pepper if needed.
10. Serve the Mediterranean tomato basil sauce over pasta, vegetables, or use it as a base for other dishes like lasagna or stuffed peppers.

11. Garnish with additional fresh basil leaves before serving (optional).

## NUTRITIONAL VALUES (per serving - approximate):

Calories: 150

Carbs: 20g

Protein: 5g

Fat: 10g

~~~~~~~~~~

# ZUCCHINI NOODLES WITH PESTO

**SERVINGS**: 2

**DIFFICULTY**: Easy

PREPARATION TIME: 10 minutes

COOKING TIME: 5 minutes

## INGREDIENTS:

- 2-3 zucchinis (about 2 pounds)
- 1/2 cup pesto (store-bought or homemade)
- Salt and freshly ground black pepper, to taste
- Optional additions:
- 1/4 cup cherry or grape tomatoes, halved
- 1/4 cup crumbled feta cheese
- 1/4 cup toasted pine nuts
- Red pepper flakes (for a little spice)

## INSTRUCTIONS:

Prepare the zucchini noodles:
1. Wash and trim the ends of the zucchini.
2. Using a spiralizer (or julienne peeler or mandoline), create zucchini noodles.
3. Place the zucchini noodles in a colander and sprinkle with a little salt. Let them sit for 10-15 minutes. This will help to draw out any excess moisture.
Cook the zucchini noodles:
4. Heat a large skillet or pan over medium heat. You can add a drizzle of olive oil if desired, but it's not necessary since zucchini releases some moisture while cooking.
5. Once hot, add the zucchini noodles and cook for 2-3 minutes, or until slightly softened and translucent. Don't overcook, or they will become mushy.
6. Using tongs, toss the noodles occasionally to ensure even cooking.
Combine with pesto:
7. Add the pesto to the pan with the cooked zucchini noodles.
8. Toss to coat the noodles evenly with the pesto.
9. Heat for an additional minute or two, just until warmed through.
Serve:
10. Season with salt and freshly ground black pepper to taste.
11. Divide the zucchini noodles with pesto among plates.
12. Top with your desired optional additions, such as cherry tomatoes, feta cheese, toasted pine nuts, or a sprinkle of red pepper flakes for a bit of spice.

## NUTRITIONAL VALUES (per 100 grams):

Calories: 100-150

Carbs: 5-10g (mostly from the zucchini)

Protein: 4-6g (mostly from the pesto)

Fat: 5-8g (mostly from the pesto and olive oil)

# DESSERT

# GRILLED FRUIT
# WITH CINNAMON

**SERVINGS**: 1

**DIFFICULTY**: Easy

**PREPARATION TIME**: 10 min.;
**COOKING TIME**: 10 min.

## INGREDIENTS:

* 1 cup assorted fruit, such as pineapple, peaches, and bananas, sliced (100g)

* 1/4 teaspoon cinnamon (1.25g)

## INSTRUCTIONS:

1. Preheat grill to medium heat.

2. Brush the fruit slices with cinnamon.

3. Grill the fruit slices for 2-3 min. per side, or until tender.

4. Serve immediately.

## NUTRITIONAL VALUES (per 100 gr.):

Calories: 50

Carbs: 10g

Protein: 1g

Fat: 0g

# BAKED APPLES
# WITH OAT CRUMBLE

**SERVINGS**: 1

**DIFFICULTY**: Easy

**PREPARATION TIME**: 10 min.;
**COOKING TIME**: 25 min.

## INGREDIENTS:

* 1 apple, cored and sliced (100g)

* 1/4 cup rolled oats (25g)

* 1 tablespoon ground cinnamon (5g)

* 1 tablespoon brown sugar (15g)

* 1 tablespoon melted butter (15g)

## INSTRUCTIONS:

1. Preheat oven to 350 degrees F (175 degrees C).

2. Place the apple slices in a small baking dish.

3. In a small bowl, combine the oats, cinnamon, brown sugar, and melted butter.

4. Sprinkle the oat crumble over the apple slices.

5. Bake for 25 min., or until the apples are tender and the oat crumble is golden brown.

6. Serve immediately.

## NUTRITIONAL VALUES (per 100 gr.):

Calories: 150

Carbs: 25g

Protein: 2g

Fat: 7g

# FROZEN YOGURT
# WITH BERRIES AND NUTS

**SERVINGS**: 1

**DIFFICULTY**: Easy

**PREPARATION TIME**: 5 min.;
**COOKING TIME**: 0 min.

## INGREDIENTS:

- 1/2 cup plain frozen yogurt (100g)
- 1/4 cup berries (25g)
- 1 tablespoon nuts, chopped (15g)

## INSTRUCTIONS:

1. Scoop the frozen yogurt into a bowl.
2. Top with berries and nuts.
3. Serve immediately.

## NUTRITIONAL VALUES (per 100 gr.):

Calories: 100

Carbs: 15g

Protein: 5g

Fat: 5g

# CHOCOLATE CHIA PUDDING

**SERVINGS**: 1

**DIFFICULTY**: Easy

**PREPARATION TIME**: 5 min.;
**COOKING TIME**: 0 min.

## INGREDIENTS:

1/4 cup chia seeds (25g)

1 cup unsweetened almond milk (250ml)

1 tablespoon unsweetened cocoa powder (5g)

1 teaspoon vanilla extract (5ml)

1/4 teaspoon stevia (1.25g)

## INSTRUCTIONS:

1. In a jar or bowl, combine the chia seeds, almond milk, cocoa powder, vanilla extract, and stevia.
2. Stir well.
3. Cover and refrigerate for at least 4 hours, or overnight.
4. Serve immediately.

## NUTRITIONAL VALUES (per 100 gr.):

Calories: 150

Carbs: 15g

Protein: 5g

Fat: 7g

# PEANUT BUTTER
# BANANA BITES

**SERVINGS**: 1

**DIFFICULTY**: Easy

**PREPARATION TIME**: 5 min.;
**COOKING TIME**: 0 min.

## INGREDIENTS:

- 1 banana, sliced (100g)

- 2 tablespoons peanut butter (30g)

## INSTRUCTIONS:

1. Spread peanut butter on one side of each banana slice.

2. Sandwich the banana slices together.

3. Serve immediately or chill for later.

## NUTRITIONAL VALUES (per 100 gr.):

Calories: 200

Carbs: 10g

Protein: 10g

Fat: 15g

# GREEK YOGURT PARFAIT
# WITH BERRIES AND GRANOLA

**SERVINGS**: 1

**DIFFICULTY**: Easy

**PREPARATION TIME**: 5 min.;
**COOKING TIME**: 0 min.

## INGREDIENTS:

- 1/2 cup plain Greek yogurt (100g)
- 1/4 cup berries (25g)
- 1/4 cup granola

## INSTRUCTIONS:

1. Layer the yogurt, berries, and granola in a glass or jar.

2. Serve immediately.

## NUTRITIONAL VALUES (per 100 gr.):

Calories: 150

Carbs: 15g

Protein: 10g

Fat: 5g

## BAKED PEARS WITH CINNAMON AND HONEY

**SERVINGS**: 1

**DIFFICULTY**: Easy

**PREPARATION TIME**: 10 min.;
**COOKING TIME**: 20 min.

### INGREDIENTS:

- 1 pear, cored and halved (100g)
- 1/4 teaspoon cinnamon (1.25g)
- 1/2 teaspoon honey (2.5g)

### INSTRUCTIONS:

1. Preheat oven to 350 degrees F (175 degrees C).

2. Place the pear halves in a small baking dish.

3. Sprinkle with cinnamon and drizzle with honey.

4. Bake for 20 min., or until the pears are tender.

5. Serve immediately.

### NUTRITIONAL VALUES (per 100 gr.):

Calories: 100

Carbs: 25g

Protein: 1g

Fat: 0g

## FRESH FRUIT SALAD WITH LIME

**SERVINGS**: 1

**DIFFICULTY**: Easy

**PREPARATION TIME**: 10 min.;
**COOKING TIME**: 0 min.

### INGREDIENTS:

- 1 cup assorted fruit, such as berries, melon, and grapes, chopped (100g)
- 1 tablespoon chopped mint leaves (5g)
- 1 tablespoon lime juice (15ml)

### INSTRUCTIONS:

1. In a bowl, combine the fruit, mint leaves, and lime juice.

2. Toss to coat.

3. Serve immediately.

### NUTRITIONAL VALUES (per 100 gr.):

Calories: 50

Carbs: 10g

Protein: 1g

Fat: 0g

# YOGURT BARK WITH BERRIES AND NUTS

**SERVINGS**: 1

**DIFFICULTY**: Easy

**PREPARATION TIME**: 10 min.;
**COOKING TIME**: 0 min.

## INGREDIENTS:

1/2 cup plain Greek yogurt (100g)

1/4 cup berries (25g)

1 tablespoon nuts, chopped (15g)

## INSTRUCTIONS:

1. Line a baking sheet with parchment paper.

2. Spread the yogurt in a thin layer on the baking sheet.

3. Sprinkle with berries and nuts.

4. Freeze for at least 30 min., or until solid.

5. Break the yogurt bark into pieces.

6. Serve immediately.

## NUTRITIONAL VALUES (per 100 gr.):

Calories: 150

Carbs: 15g

Protein: 10g

Fat: 5g

# CHIA SEED PUDDING WITH FRUIT AND YOGURT

**SERVINGS**: 1

**DIFFICULTY**: Easy

**PREPARATION TIME**: 5 min.;
**COOKING TIME**: 0 min.

## INGREDIENTS:

- 1/4 cup chia seeds (25g)
- 1 cup unsweetened almond milk (250ml)
- 1/4 cup fruit, chopped (25g)
- 1/4 cup plain Greek yogurt (60g)

## INSTRUCTIONS:

1. In a jar or bowl, combine the chia seeds and almond milk.

2. Stir well.

3. Cover and refrigerate for at least 4 hours, or overnight.

4. Stir in the fruit and yogurt.

5. Serve immediately.

## NUTRITIONAL VALUES (per 100 gr.):

Calories: 150

Carbs: 15g

Protein: 10g

Fat: 5g

# FROZEN FRUIT POPS

**SERVINGS**: 1

**DIFFICULTY**: Easy

**PREPARATION TIME**: 10 min.;
**COOKING TIME**: 0 min.

## INGREDIENTS:

- 1 cup assorted fruit, such as berries, melon, and grapes, chopped (100g)
- 1/4 cup unsweetened almond milk (60ml)

## INSTRUCTIONS:

1. In a blender, combine the fruit and almond milk.

2. Blend until smooth.

3. Pour the mixture into popsicle molds.

4. Freeze for at least 4 hours, or until solid.

5. Serve immediately.

## NUTRITIONAL VALUES (per 100 gr.):

Calories: 50

Carbs: 10g

Protein: 1g

Fat: 0g

# BAKED APPLES WITH QUINOA AND NUTS

**SERVINGS**: 1

**DIFFICULTY**: Easy

**PREPARATION TIME**: 10 min.;
**COOKING TIME**: 25 min.

## INGREDIENTS:

- 1 apple, cored and halved (100g)

- 1/4 cup cooked quinoa (25g)

- 1 tablespoon nuts, chopped (15g)

- 1/4 teaspoon cinnamon (1.25g)

- 1/4 teaspoon nutmeg (1.25g)

- 1/4 teaspoon stevia (1.25g)

## INSTRUCTIONS:

1. Preheat oven to 350 degrees F (175 degrees C).

2. Place the apple halves in a small baking dish.

3. Stuff the apple halves with the quinoa, nuts, cinnamon, nutmeg, and stevia.

4. Bake for 25 min., or until the apples are tender.

5. Serve immediately.

## NUTRITIONAL VALUES (per 100 gr.):

Calories: 200

Carbs: 30g

Protein: 10g

Fat: 5g

# GREEK YOGURT PARFAIT WITH BERRIES AND GRANOLA

**SERVINGS**: 1

**DIFFICULTY**: Easy

**PREPARATION TIME**: 5 min.;
**COOKING TIME**: 0 min.

## INGREDIENTS:

- 1/2 cup plain Greek yogurt (100g)
- 1/4 cup berries (25g)
- 1/4 cup granola (25g)

## INSTRUCTIONS:

1. In a glass or jar, layer the yogurt, berries, and granola.
2. Repeat the layers until the glass or jar is full.
3. Serve immediately.

## NUTRITIONAL VALUES (per 100 gr.):

Calories: 150

Carbs: 15g

Protein: 10g

Fat: 5g

# BAKED PEACHES WITH CINNAMON AND YOGURT

**SERVINGS**: 1

**DIFFICULTY**: Easy

**PREPARATION TIME**: 10 min.;
**COOKING TIME**: 20 min.

## INGREDIENTS:

- 1 peach, halved and pitted (100g)
- 1/4 teaspoon cinnamon (1.25g)
- 1/4 cup plain Greek yogurt (60g)

## INSTRUCTIONS:

1. Preheat oven to 350 degrees F (175 degrees C).
2. Place the peach halves in a small baking dish.
3. Sprinkle with cinnamon.
4. Bake for 20 min., or until the peaches are tender.
5. Serve with Greek yogurt.

## NUTRITIONAL VALUES (per 100 gr.):

Calories: 150

Carbs: 25g

Protein: 10g

Fat: 5g

# ROASTED PEARS WITH HONEY AND WALNUTS

**SERVINGS**: 1

**DIFFICULTY**: Easy

**PREPARATION TIME**: 10 min.;
**COOKING TIME**: 25 min.

## INGREDIENTS:

- 1 pear, halved and cored (100g)
- 1/2 teaspoon honey (2.5g)
- 1 tablespoon walnuts, chopped (15g)

## INSTRUCTIONS:

1. Preheat oven to 350 degrees F (175 degrees C).
2. Place the pear halves in a small baking dish.
3. Drizzle with honey and sprinkle with walnuts.
4. Bake for 25 min., or until the pears are tender.
5. Serve immediately.

## NUTRITIONAL VALUES (per 100 gr.):

Calories: 200

Carbs: 30g

Protein: 5g

Fat: 15g

# FROZEN YOGURT BITES WITH BERRIES AND NUTS

**SERVINGS**: 1

**DIFFICULTY**: Easy

**PREPARATION TIME**: 10 min.;
**Freezing time:** At least 4 hours

## INGREDIENTS:

- 1/2 cup plain Greek yogurt (100g)
- 1/4 cup berries (25g)
- 1 tablespoon nuts, chopped (15g)

## INSTRUCTIONS:

1. Line a baking sheet with parchment paper.
2. Spoon the yogurt onto the baking sheet, forming small balls.
3. Top with berries and nuts.
4. Freeze for at least 4 hours, or until solid.
5. Serve immediately.

## NUTRITIONAL VALUES (per 100 gr.):

Calories: 150

Carbs: 15g

Protein: 10g

Fat: 5g

# DARK CHOCOLATE AVOCADO MOUSSE

**SERVINGS**: 1

**DIFFICULTY**: Easy

**PREPARATION TIME**: 10 min.

## INGREDIENTS:

- 1/2 avocado, peeled and pitted (50g)
- 1/4 cup unsweetened cocoa powder (25g)
- 1 tablespoon honey (15g)
- 1/4 cup unsweetened almond milk (60ml)

## INSTRUCTIONS:

1. In a blender, combine the avocado, cocoa powder, honey, and almond milk.
2. Blend until smooth.
3. Pour the mousse into a **SERVING** glass or bowl.
4. Serve immediately.

## NUTRITIONAL VALUES (per 100 gr.):

Calories: 200

Carbs: 15g

Protein: 5g

Fat: 15g

# BANANA NUT MUFFINS

**SERVINGS**: 1

**DIFFICULTY**: Easy

**PREPARATION TIME**: 10 min.; Baking time: 20 min.

## INGREDIENTS:

- 1/2 cup whole-wheat flour (50g)
- 1/4 cup rolled oats (25g)
- 1/4 teaspoon baking powder (1.25g)
- 1/4 teaspoon baking soda (1.25g)
- 1/4 teaspoon salt (1.25g)
- 1/4 cup mashed ripe banana (50g)
- 1/4 cup unsweetened almond milk (60ml)
- 1 tablespoon melted coconut oil (15ml)
- 1 tablespoon chopped walnuts (15g)

## INSTRUCTIONS:

1. Preheat oven to 350 degrees F (175 degrees C).
2. Grease a muffin tin with coconut oil or cooking spray.
3. In a bowl, combine the flour, oats, baking powder, baking soda, and salt.
4. In a separate bowl, combine the banana, almond milk, and melted coconut oil.
5. Add the wet **ingredients** to the dry **ingredients** and mix until just combined.
6. Fold in the walnuts.
7. Pour the batter into the prepared muffin tin.
8. Bake for 20 min., or until a toothpick inserted into the center of a muffin comes out clean.

9. Let the muffins cool in the pan for a few min. before removing them to a wire rack to cool completely.

## NUTRITIONAL VALUES (per 100 gr.):

Calories: 200

Carbs: 30g

Protein: 5g

Fat: 10g

~~~~~~~~~~~~~~~

## CINNAMON BALLS

**SERVINGS**: Varies depending on size (estimate 12-15)

**DIFFICULTY**: Easy

**PREPARATION TIME**: 15 minutes

**COOKING TIME**: 10-12 minutes

## INGREDIENTS:

- Dry ingredients (mixture of flour, cinnamon, and other baking staples)
- Wet ingredients (binding agent like eggs and additional flavorings)
- Fat (butter, oil, or shortening)
- Coating (cinnamon sugar mixture)

## INSTRUCTIONS:

1. Preheat oven to a designated temperature (usually around 375°F / 190°C).
2. In a large bowl, combine dry ingredients (flour, cinnamon, etc.).
3. In a separate bowl, whisk together wet ingredients (eggs, flavorings).
4. Gradually incorporate the wet ingredients into the dry ingredients, mixing until a soft dough forms.
5. If using, add fat (butter, oil, etc.) to the dough and mix until well-combined.
6. Shape the dough into small balls (size may vary depending on desired outcome).
7. Prepare the coating by combining sugar and cinnamon in a shallow dish.
8. Roll each dough ball in the cinnamon sugar mixture to coat evenly.
9. Place the coated balls on a baking sheet lined with parchment paper.
10. Bake for the designated time (around 10-12 minutes) or until golden brown.
11. Let the balls cool slightly before serving.

## NUTRITIONAL VALUES (per serving - approximate):

Calories: (will vary depending on ingredients and size)

Carbs: (high)

Protein: (low)

Fat: (moderate)

~~~~~~~~~~~~~~~

## LEMON COCONUT MUFFINS

**SERVINGS**: 12

**DIFFICULTY**: Easy

**PREPARATION TIME**: 15 minutes

**COOKING TIME**: 20-25 minutes

## INGREDIENTS:

- 1 1/2 cups all-purpose flour
- 1/2 cup unsweetened shredded coconut
- 1 1/2 teaspoons baking powder
- 1/2 teaspoon baking soda
- 1/4 teaspoon salt
- 1/2 cup (1 stick) unsalted butter, softened
- 3/4 cup granulated sugar
- 2 large eggs
- 1 teaspoon grated lemon zest
- 1/4 cup freshly squeezed lemon juice
- 1/2 cup buttermilk (or milk with 1 tablespoon vinegar added)

## INSTRUCTIONS:

1. Preheat oven to 375°F (190°C). Line a muffin tin with paper liners.

2. In a medium bowl, whisk together flour, shredded coconut, baking powder, baking soda, and salt.
3. In a large bowl, cream together softened butter and sugar until light and fluffy.
4. Beat in eggs one at a time, then stir in lemon zest and lemon juice.
5. Alternately add the dry ingredients and buttermilk to the wet ingredients, mixing until just combined. Don't overmix.
6. Fill the prepared muffin cups batter, leaving a little space at the top for muffins to rise.
7. Bake for 20-25 minutes, or until a toothpick inserted into the center comes out clean.
8. Let the muffins cool in the pan for a few minutes before transferring them to a wire rack to cool completely.

## NUTRITIONAL VALUES (per muffin - approximate):

Calories: 300

Carbs: 40g

Protein: 4g

Fat: 15g

# SMOOTHIES

# BERRY BLAST SMOOTHIE

**SERVING**: 1

**DIFFICULTY**: Easy

TIME NEEDED: **PREPARATION TIME**: 5 min.

## INGREDIENTS:

- 1 cup frozen mixed berries (100g)
- 1/2 cup unsweetened almond milk (125ml)
- 1/4 cup plain Greek yogurt (60g)
- 1 tablespoon chia seeds (15g)

## INSTRUCTIONS:

1. Combine all **ingredients** in a blender and blend until smooth.
2. Serve immediately.

## NUTRITIONAL VALUES:

Calories: 150

Carbs: 15g

Protein: 10g

Fat: 5g

# GREEN GODDESS SMOOTHIE

**SERVING**: 1

**DIFFICULTY**: Easy

TIME NEEDED: **PREPARATION TIME**: 5 min.

## INGREDIENTS:

- 1 cup spinach (50g)
- 1/2 cup kale (50g)
- 1/2 avocado, peeled and pitted (50g)
- 1/2 banana (50g)
- 1/2 cup unsweetened almond milk (125ml)

## INSTRUCTIONS:

1. Combine all **ingredients** in a blender and blend until smooth.
2. Serve immediately.

## NUTRITIONAL VALUES:

Calories: 200

Carbs: 15g

Protein: 5g

Fat: 15g

# TROPICAL TURMERIC SMOOTHIE

**SERVING**: 1

**DIFFICULTY**: Easy

TIME NEEDED: **PREPARATION TIME**: 5 min.

## INGREDIENTS:

- 1 cup frozen mango (100g)
- 1/2 cup pineapple chunks (100g)
- 1/2 cup unsweetened coconut milk (125ml)
- 1/2 teaspoon ground turmeric (2.5g)
- 1/4 teaspoon ground cinnamon (1.25g)

## INSTRUCTIONS:

1. Combine all **ingredients** in a blender and blend until smooth.

## NUTRITIONAL VALUES:

Calories: 200

Carbs: 30g

Protein: 5g

Fat: 10g

# BERRY BEET SMOOTHIE

**SERVING**: 1

**DIFFICULTY**: Easy

TIME NEEDED: **PREPARATION TIME**: 5 min.

## INGREDIENTS:

- 1 cup frozen mixed berries (100g)
- 1/2 cup cooked beets, chopped (100g)
- 1/2 cup unsweetened almond milk (125ml)
- 1/4 teaspoon ground cinnamon (1.25g)

## INSTRUCTIONS:

1. Combine all **ingredients** in a blender and blend until smooth.

Optional: Add 1 tablespoon of chia seeds or ground flaxseed for a boost of fiber and omega-3 fatty acids.

## NUTRITIONAL VALUES:

Calories: 150

Carbs: 15g

Protein: 5g

Fat: 5g

# AVOCADO MATCHA SMOOTHIE

**SERVING**: 1

**DIFFICULTY**: Easy

TIME NEEDED: **PREPARATION TIME**: 5 min.

## INGREDIENTS:

- 1/2 avocado, peeled and pitted (50g)
- 1/2 cup unsweetened almond milk (125ml)
- 1 teaspoon matcha powder (5g)
- 1/4 teaspoon ground cinnamon (1.25g)
- 1/4 teaspoon ground ginger (1.25g)

## INSTRUCTIONS:

1. Combine all ingredients in a blender and blend until smooth.

## NUTRITIONAL VALUES:

Calories: 200

Carbs: 15g

Protein: 5g

Fat: 15g

# CHOCOLATE PEANUT BUTTER SMOOTHIE

**SERVING**: 1

**DIFFICULTY**: Easy

TIME NEEDED: **PREPARATION TIME**: 5 min.

## INGREDIENTS:

- 1/2 cup frozen berries (100g)
- 1/2 banana (50g)
- 1 tablespoon peanut butter (15g)
- 1 tablespoon unsweetened cocoa powder (5g)
- 1 cup unsweetened almond milk (250ml)

## INSTRUCTIONS:

1. Combine all **ingredients** in a blender and blend until smooth.
2. Serve immediately.

## NUTRITIONAL VALUES:

Calories: 200

Carbs: 20g

Protein: 10g

Fat: 10g

# GREEN TEA SMOOTHIE WITH MINT AND GINGER

**SERVING**: 1

**DIFFICULTY**:

TIME NEEDED: **PREPARATION TIME**: 5 min.

**INGREDIENTS**:

- 1 cup spinach (50g)
- 1/2 cup kale (50g)
- 1/2 avocado, peeled and pitted (50g)
- 1 cup unsweetened green tea (250ml)
- 1 tablespoon chopped mint
- 1/4 teaspoon ground ginger (1.25g)

**INSTRUCTIONS**:

1. Combine all **ingredients** in a blender and blend until smooth.

**NUTRITIONAL VALUES**:

Calories: 200

Carbs: 15g

Protein: 5g

Fat: 15g

# PINEAPPLE MANGO TANGO SMOOTHIE

**SERVING**: 1

**DIFFICULTY**: Easy

TIME NEEDED: **PREPARATION TIME**: 5 min.

**INGREDIENTS**:

- 1 cup frozen pineapple chunks (100g)
- 1 cup frozen mango chunks (100g)
- 1/2 cup unsweetened coconut milk (125ml)
- 1/4 teaspoon ground turmeric (1.25g)

**INSTRUCTIONS**:

1. Combine all **ingredients** in a blender and blend until smooth.
2. Serve immediately.

**NUTRITIONAL VALUES**:

Calories: 200

Carbs: 30g

Protein: 5g

Fat: 10g

# BLUEBERRY ALMOND SMOOTHIE

**SERVING**: 1

**DIFFICULTY**: Easy

TIME NEEDED: **PREPARATION TIME**: 5 min.

## INGREDIENTS:

- 1 cup frozen blueberries (100g)
- 1/2 avocado, peeled and pitted (50g)
- 1/2 cup unsweetened almond milk (125ml)
- 1/4 teaspoon ground cinnamon (1.25g)

## INSTRUCTIONS:

1. Combine all **ingredients** in a blender and blend until smooth.
2. Serve immediately.

## NUTRITIONAL VALUES:

Calories: 200

Carbs: 15g

Protein: 5g

Fat: 15g

# COFFEE CHIA SMOOTHIE

**SERVING**: 1

**DIFFICULTY**: Easy

TIME NEEDED: **PREPARATION TIME**: 5 min.

## INGREDIENTS:

- 1/2 cup unsweetened cold coffee (125ml)
- 1/2 banana (50g)
- 1 tablespoon chia seeds (15g)
- 1/4 teaspoon ground cinnamon (1.25g)

## INSTRUCTIONS:

1. Combine all **ingredients** in a blender and blend until smooth.
2. Serve immediately.

## NUTRITIONAL VALUES:

Calories: 150

Carbs: 15g

Protein: 5g

Fat: 5g

# PEANUT BUTTER AND JELLY SMOOTHIE

**SERVING**: 1

**DIFFICULTY**: Easy

TIME NEEDED: **PREPARATION TIME**: 5 min.

## INGREDIENTS:

- 1/2 cup unsweetened almond milk (125 ml)
- 1/4 cup frozen raspberries (25 g)
- 1/4 cup frozen strawberries (25 g)
- 1 tablespoon peanut butter (15 g)
- 1 teaspoon unsweetened cocoa powder (5 g)

## INSTRUCTIONS:

1. Combine all **ingredients** in a blender and blend until smooth.
2. Serve immediately.

## NUTRITIONAL VALUES:

Calories: 200

Carbs: 20 g

Protein: 10 g

Fat: 10 g

# GREEN TEA SMOOTHIE WITH MINT AND CUCUMBER

**SERVING**: 1

**DIFFICULTY**: Easy

TIME NEEDED: **PREPARATION TIME**: 5 min.

## INGREDIENTS:

- 1 cup unsweetened green tea (250 ml)
- 1/2 cup spinach (50 g)
- 1/2 cucumber, peeled and sliced (50 g)
- 1 tablespoon chopped mint
- 1/4 teaspoon ground ginger (1.25 g)

## INSTRUCTIONS:

1. Combine all **ingredients** in a blender and blend until smooth.
2. Serve immediately.

## NUTRITIONAL VALUES:

Calories: 50

Carbs: 10 g

Protein: 1 g

Fat: 0 g

# MANGO AVOCADO SMOOTHIE

**SERVING**: 1

**DIFFICULTY**: Easy

TIME NEEDED: **PREPARATION TIME**: 5 min.

## INGREDIENTS:

- 1/2 cup frozen mango chunks (50 g)
- 1/2 avocado, peeled and pitted (50 g)
- 1/2 cup unsweetened almond milk (125 ml)
- 1/4 teaspoon ground turmeric (1.25 g)

## INSTRUCTIONS:

1. Combine all ingredients in a blender and blend until smooth.
2. Serve immediately.

## NUTRITIONAL VALUES:

- Calories: 200
- Carbs: 15 g
- Protein: 5 g
- Fat: 15 g

# BERRY BANANA BLAST SMOOTHIE

**SERVING**: 1

**DIFFICULTY**: Easy

TIME NEEDED: **PREPARATION TIME**: 5 min.

## INGREDIENTS:

- 1 cup frozen mixed berries (100 g)
- 1/2 banana (50 g)
- 1/2 cup unsweetened almond milk (125 ml)
- 1 tablespoon chia seeds (15 g)

## INSTRUCTIONS:

1. Combine all **ingredients** in a blender and blend until smooth.
2. Serve immediately.

## NUTRITIONAL VALUES:

- Calories: 150
- Carbs: 15 g
- Protein: 5 g
- Fat: 5 g

# GREEN POWER SMOOTHIE

**SERVING**: 1

**DIFFICULTY**: Easy

TIME NEEDED: **PREPARATION TIME**: 5 min.

## INGREDIENTS:

- 1 cup spinach (50 g)
- 1/2 cup kale (50 g)
- 1/2 avocado, peeled and pitted (50 g)
- 1/2 banana (50 g)
- 1/2 cup unsweetened almond milk (125 ml)
- 1 tablespoon ground flaxseed (7.5 g)

## INSTRUCTIONS:

1. Combine all **ingredients** in a blender and blend until smooth.
2. Serve immediately.

## NUTRITIONAL VALUES:

- Calories: 200
- Carbs: 15 g
- Protein: 5 g
- Fat: 15 g

# CONCLUSION

In conclusion, our liver is a vital organ responsible for many important functions in our body, including detoxification. However, in today's modern lifestyle, our liver can easily become overburdened with toxins, leading to various liver diseases such as fatty liver disease. This guide has provided information on how to detoxify and cleanse the liver naturally, along with a comprehensive list of foods to avoid, moderate consumption, and foods allowed. We also provided a variety of delicious and healthy recipes for breakfast, lunch, dinner, side dishes, and smoothies that can help support a healthy liver. Additionally, a 3-week meal plan has been included to help you put this information into practice. By making small changes to our diet and lifestyle, we can support the health of our liver and overall well-being.

**Did you enjoy the book? 🎉 If it added a sprinkle of flavor to your meals or made your healthy eating journey a little easier, we'd love to hear about it! Your review on Amazon helps others discover this diet and join the health revolution. Plus, it makes our day! 🎇 Thank you for your support—you're awesome!"**

## SCAN THE FOLLOWING CODE!

**Thank you!**

# 30-DAY MEAL PLAN

## Week 1

| Day | Breakfast | Lunch | Dinner | Side Dish | Dessert |
|---|---|---|---|---|---|
| Monday | Oatmeal with Berries and Nuts (34) | Grilled Salmon with Roasted Vegetables (45) | Lentil Soup (45) | Roasted Zucchini (56) | Greek Yogurt Parfait (63) |
| Tuesday | Yogurt Parfait with Fruit and Granola (34) | Quinoa Salad with Roasted Veg & Chickpeas (46) | Black Bean Burgers with Sweet Potato Fries (50) | Steamed Green Beans (56) | no |
| Wednesday | Smoothie with Berries, Spinach, & Yogurt (35) | Chicken and Vegetable Stir-Fry (47) | Tuna Steaks with Avocado (52) | Roasted Tomatoes (57) | Baked Pears with Cinnamon & Honey (64) |
| Thursday | Whole-Wheat Toast with Avocado & Eggs (35) | Lentil and Vegetable Curry (46) | Shrimp and Broccoli Stir-Fry (53) | Mashed Cauliflower (57) | no |
| Friday | Scrambled Eggs with Vegetables (37) | Tuna and Walnut Salad (49) | Grilled Shrimp with Roasted Vegetables (49) | Roasted Red Peppers (58) | no |
| Saturday | Chia Pudding with Berries and Nuts (36) | Tofu Scramble with Vegetables (47) | Turkey Meatballs with Spaghetti Squash (48) | Zucchini Noodles with Pesto (59) | no |
| Sunday | Whole-Wheat Waffles with Peanut Butter & Banana (36) | Quinoa Salad with Chickpeas & Avocado (50) | Spicy Ginger Chicken (52) | Roasted Carrots (55) | Fresh Fruit Salad with Lime (64) |

# Week 2

| Day | Breakfast | Lunch | Dinner | Side Dish | Dessert |
|---|---|---|---|---|---|
| Monday | Smoothie with Spinach, Kale, & Banana (42) | Grilled Salmon with Roasted Vegetables (45) | Lentil and Vegetable Soup (51) | Steamed Green Beans (56) | Baked Apples with Quinoa & Nuts (66) |
| Tuesday | Whole-Wheat Toast with Avocado & Tomatoes (39) | Chicken and Brown Rice Stir-Fry (55) | Shrimp and Broccoli Stir-Fry (53) | Mashed Cauliflower (57) | no |
| Wednesday | Cottage Cheese with Berries and Nuts (40) | Quinoa Salad with Roasted Vegetables (46) | Turkey Meatballs with Spaghetti Squash (48) | Roasted Tomatoes (57) | Frozen Yogurt Bites with Berries (68) |
| Thursday | Hard-Boiled Eggs with Fruit and Nuts (39) | Tofu Scramble with Vegetables (47) | Grilled Shrimp with Roasted Vegetables (49) | Roasted Zucchini (56) | no |
| Friday | Smoothie with Avocado, Banana, & Spinach (40) | Tuna and Walnut Salad (49) | Black Bean Burgers with Sweet Potato Fries (50) | Roasted Red Peppers (58) | no |
| Saturday | Quinoa Porridge with Berries and Nuts (41) | Lentil Soup (45) | Tuna Steaks with Avocado (52) | Roasted Carrots (55) | no |
| Sunday | Whole-Wheat Pancakes with Apples & Cinnamon (41) | Lentil and Vegetable Curry (46) | Spicy Ginger Chicken (52) | Zucchini Noodles with Pesto (59) | Roasted Pears with Honey & Walnuts (68) |

# Week 3

| Day | Breakfast | Lunch | Dinner | Side Dish | Dessert |
|---|---|---|---|---|---|
| Monday | Smoothie with Avocado, Banana, & Berries (43) | Grilled Salmon with Roasted Vegetables (45) | Lentil Soup (45) | Roasted Zucchini (56) | no |
| Tuesday | Yogurt Parfait with Granola and Nuts (38) | Quinoa Salad with Chickpeas & Avocado (50) | Black Bean Burgers with Sweet Potato Fries (50) | Steamed Green Beans (56) | no |
| Wednesday | Oatmeal with Peanut Butter and Chia Seeds (37) | Tuna and Walnut Salad (49) | Spicy Ginger Chicken (52) | Mashed Cauliflower (57) | no |
| Thursday | Whole-Wheat Pancakes with Apples & Cinnamon (41) | Tofu Scramble with Vegetables (47) | Grilled Shrimp with Roasted Vegetables (49) | Roasted Tomatoes (57) | Dark Chocolate Avocado Mousse (69) |
| Friday | Smoothie with Spinach, Kale, and Banana (42) | Chicken and Vegetable Stir-Fry (47) | Turkey Meatballs with Spaghetti Squash (48) | Roasted Carrots (55) | no |
| Saturday | Cottage Cheese with Berries and Nuts (40) | Lentil Soup (45) | Shrimp and Broccoli Stir-Fry (53) | Roasted Red Peppers (58) | Frozen Yogurt Bites with Berries (68) |
| Sunday | Whole-Wheat Waffles with Peanut Butter & Banana (36) | Lentil and Vegetable Curry (46) | Tuna Steaks with Avocado (52) | Zucchini Noodles with Pesto (59) | Fresh Fruit Salad with Lime (64) |

# Week 4

| Day | Breakfast | Lunch | Dinner | Side Dish | Dessert |
|---|---|---|---|---|---|
| Monday | Quinoa Porridge with Berries and Nuts (41) | Grilled Salmon with Roasted Vegetables (45) | Lentil Soup (45) | Roasted Tomatoes (57) | no |
| Tuesday | Yogurt Parfait with Fruit and Granola (34) | Tofu Scramble with Vegetables (47) | Turkey Meatballs with Spaghetti Squash (48) | Steamed Green Beans (56) | Cinnamon Balls (70) |
| Wednesday | Smoothie with Avocado, Banana, & Spinach (40) | Tuna and Walnut Salad (49) | Spicy Ginger Chicken (52) | Mashed Cauliflower (57) | no |
| Thursday | Cottage Cheese with Berries and Nuts (40) | Lentil and Vegetable Curry (46) | Grilled Shrimp with Roasted Vegetables (49) | Roasted Zucchini (56) | Frozen Yogurt Bites with Berries (68) |
| Friday | Whole-Wheat Toast with Avocado & Eggs (35) | Chicken and Brown Rice Stir-Fry (55) | Tuna Steaks with Avocado (52) | Roasted Red Peppers (58) | no |
| Saturday | Oatmeal with Berries and Nuts (34) | Quinoa Salad with Roasted Veg & Chickpeas (46) | Shrimp and Broccoli Stir-Fry (53) | Roasted Carrots (55) | no |
| Sunday | Whole-Wheat Waffles with Peanut Butter & Banana (36) | Lentil Soup (45) | Black Bean Burgers with Sweet Potato Fries (50) | Zucchini Noodles with Pesto (59) | Fresh Fruit Salad with Lime (64) |

# Week 5

| Day | Breakfast | Lunch | Dinner | Side Dish | Dessert |
|---|---|---|---|---|---|
| Monday | Smoothie with Berries, Spinach, & Yogurt (35) | Grilled Salmon with Roasted Vegetables (45) | Lentil and Vegetable Soup (51) | Steamed Green Beans (56) | no |
| Tuesday | Chia Pudding with Berries and Nuts (36) | Chicken and Brown Rice Stir-Fry (55) | Turkey Meatballs with Spaghetti Squash (48) | Mashed Cauliflower (57) | no |
| Wednesday | Whole-Wheat Toast with Avocado & Tomatoes (39) | Quinoa Salad with Chickpeas & Avocado (50) | Spicy Ginger Chicken (52) | Roasted Zucchini (56) | Baked Apples with Quinoa & Nuts (66) |
| Thursday | Scrambled Eggs with Vegetables (37) | Tuna and Walnut Salad (49) | Shrimp and Broccoli Stir-Fry (53) | Roasted Tomatoes (57) | no |
| Friday | Oatmeal with Berries and Yogurt (42) | Lentil and Vegetable Curry (46) | Grilled Shrimp with Roasted Vegetables (49) | Roasted Carrots (55) | Frozen Yogurt with Berries (62) |
| Saturday | Hard-Boiled Eggs with Fruit and Nuts (39) | Lentil Soup (45) | Tuna Steaks with Avocado (52) | Zucchini Noodles with Pesto (59) | no |
| Sunday | Whole-Wheat Pancakes with Apples & Cinnamon (41) | Chicken and Vegetable Stir-Fry (47) | Black Bean Burgers with Sweet Potato Fries (50) | Roasted Red Peppers (58) | no |

# BONUS ALERT

These bonus resources are designed to complement your cookbook and enhance your overall health and fitness journey. Scan the codes to access these valuable PDFs and take your wellness routine,

## READING FOOD LABELS

A simple guide to reading food labels. Empower yourself to make informed choices about the food you eat.

## 1-YEAR DIET JOURNAL

A 1-year journal: Track your progress, document your experiences, and celebrate your achievements.

# HIIT (HIGH-INTENSITY INTERVAL TRAINING)

Get ready to supercharge your fitness journey with our HIIT guide! High-Intensity Interval Training is a fantastic way to boost your metabolism, burn calories, and get your heart pumping. Whether you're a beginner or a seasoned fitness enthusiast, this comprehensive PDF will provide you with valuable insights, exercise routines, and tips to maximize your HIIT workouts.

# PRACTICAL GUIDE TO STARTING TRAINING

Are you new to the world of fitness and exercise? This book is the perfect resource to kickstart your fitness journey. Inside this PDF, you'll find step-by-step instructions, workout plans, and expert advice on how to get started with a safe and effective exercise routine. It's the ideal companion for anyone looking to build a strong foundation for a healthier lifestyle.

# MINDFULNESS AND EXERCISE

Achieve holistic well-being through the fusion of mindfulness and exercise. Our PDF on "Mindfulness and Exercise" explores the powerful connection between the mind and body. Discover techniques for staying present during your workouts and harnessing the mental benefits of exercise. This guide is your gateway to a balanced and mindful approach to fitness.

# MEDITERRANEAN DIET

# COOKBOOK FOR BEGINNERS

Discover the benefits of the Mediterranean diet with this beginner-friendly cookbook. Featuring easy recipes, meal plans, and tips, it helps you incorporate heart-healthy, flavorful dishes into your daily life. Enjoy fresh vegetables, fruits, whole grains, and lean proteins inspired by Mediterranean cuisine. Start your journey to healthier eating today!!

Made in the USA
Monee, IL
25 March 2025

14607563R00050